Want to Change the World?

Want to Change the World?

Accelerate Your Nonprofit or Cause

Tom Peterson

Stakeholder Press

BOOKS TO MAKE THE WORLD BETTER

Tom Peterson
cosmorock.org

ISBN: 978-1-7324222-1-6

Editing: Melanie Raskin

Front cover illustration: Tom Peterson

Author photograph: Ash Jackson

Cover and book design: H. K. Stewart

Printed in the United States of America

This book is printed on archival-quality paper that meets requirements of the American National Standard for Information Sciences, Permanence of Paper, Printed Library Materials, ANSI Z39.48-1984.

To **you**...

who obviously answered **Yes** to the book title

because you are now reading this.

Thanks for engaging in your

patch of world change!

And to **Walt** and **Eliot**

Contents

CHAPTER ONE

Audacious agency

As Doug Tallamy headed off to college his older brother told him, "Don't take any science because you're not smart enough for it." He took the advice for a year, but couldn't resist trying biology as a sophomore. He liked it. In his junior year, he signed up for an entomology class from, and this is true, Dr. Bugby, and Tallamy has been captivated by insects ever since. He went on to get his doctorate and has taught at the University of Delaware for four decades. In 2000, Tallamy and his wife moved to a house in Oxford, Pennsylvania with a ten-acre lot that had once been farmland. Because it hadn't been mowed for three years, invasive plants had taken over. "The entire ten acres looked like Sleeping Beauty's castle," Tallamy told me. "You couldn't walk anywhere." So the two of them began cutting trails through the property.

One day Tallamy noticed something. As an entomologist he looks for insects all the time, and you find them, he says, by seeing feeding damage on leaves. So it was what he was *not* seeing that caught his attention. "There weren't any holes on the invasive plants, but there were several on the natives that were there." Tallamy realized this would make an interesting study: Why weren't insects eating any of the invasive plants? There happened to be an undergraduate looking for a project. Her first assignment was to go to the literature to see what had already been done about measuring insect impacts on native and non-native plants. A couple days later she reported that she couldn't find anything. Well, she's an undergrad, thought Tallamy, so he looked himself. He couldn't find anything either, concluding "There's a big, long list of why invasive plants are not good for ecosystems, but wrecking the food web was not on it." A food web shows how every being on the planet (animals, plants, fungi, bacterium) impacts its habitat—it's all about food chains and who eats what.

So Tallamy and his colleagues got some grants and began to study how big a problem invasive plants were. They learned that more than 80 percent of the plants in residential neighborhoods are non-native. "It all came together that this is a major cause of bird declines, insect declines, and biodiversity declines in general," he said, "not just in this country, but around the world." Meanwhile, Tallamy began getting invited to give talks at bird clubs and garden clubs. Because many in the audience asked for more information, he started out to make a pamphlet, which turned into the book *Bringing Nature Home*. While researching for the book, Tallamy came across the statistic that there were forty million acres of lawn in the United States—an area the size of New England. *That's a lot of lawn*, he thought. *What would happen if we cut it in half?* When he added up the areas of the major national parks it still wasn't twenty million acres. So he said, "Let's create a national park at home by reducing lawns. We'll call it Homegrown National Park. So I started putting that in my talks and I talked about it for years and years."

To describe the beginnings of a movement, Derek Sivers once showed a three-minute amateur video to a TED-talk audience.[1] It starts out with a shirtless young man dancing and waving his arms at an outdoor rock concert. He's surrounded by a crowd sitting on a grassy slope listening to the music being played down the hill.

After a while, a second guy gets up and starts to dance with him. This second guy calls to his friends to join and before long most of the audience is dancing. "Leadership is over-glorified," said Sivers. "Yes, it was the shirtless guy who was first and he'll get all the credit, but it was really the first *follower* that transformed the lone nut into a leader… If you really care about starting a movement, have the courage to follow and show others how to follow." Enter Tallamy's first follower: Michelle Alfandari. For more than thirty years, Alfandari had run a New York City-based licensing and marketing agency, serving a mix of global corporate and nonprofit clients. She had no interest in gardening but had inherited a garden when she and her husband moved from The City to Sharon, Connecticut. In 2017, a neighbor suggested she go hear Tallamy talk at a local event. On that rainy day, she noticed that the audience was packed with gardeners and landscape designers hanging on to Tallamy's every word. "I was learning that there's this biodiversity crisis due to loss of habitat *and* there's a solution," Alfandari told me. "As a marketing person, I'm getting excited— not like everyone else in the audience saying, 'Oh, we'll replace that burning bush with this or that.' I saw what we call the white space, an unarticulated need that represents an opportunity."

Alfandari kept thinking about it, and in 2019, reached out to Tallamy. They agreed to meet at an upcoming symposium. "You know, you only talked to the choir," she told him when they got together. "Yeah, it's only the choir who invites me," he quipped. She went on, "But this isn't going to work unless you get beyond the choir." She was not the first person to approach Tallamy saying, "Wow, we've got to get the word out." Always booked, he said he didn't have the time, and even though Alfandari had recently committed to slowing down her work pace, together, they decided to create Homegrown National Park.

Enter *more* followers…and you have a movement. A few months ago, a note printed on a half-page of paper showed up in my mailbox: "Hi neighbor! This fall, I'm asking you to *leave the leaves!* Leaves are not litter—they're food and shelter for butterflies, beetles, bees, moths and more." The neighbor went on to describe how Luna moths and swallowtail butterflies use the leaves for shelter from predators. She listed a few things we could do and gave her email address and a website where we could learn more. That's how I learned about Homegrown National Park.

Acting audaciously

Are we now living in the prequel to a dystopian future? It's a turbulent time, a make-or-break time. A recent UN report called it "a code red for humanity" and warns that "the alarm bells are deafening, and the evidence is irrefutable: greenhouse-gas emissions from fossil-fuel burning and deforestation are choking our planet and putting billions of people at immediate risk."[2] And then there's the wealth gap: Oxfam reports that just ten men—including Elon Musk, Jeff Bezos, Mark Zuckerberg, and Bill Gates—have more combined wealth than the poorest three billion people on Earth. Autocrats are on the rise and democracy is under existential threat in the United States and around the world. Meanwhile, people of all types need help right now in every community. And billions of the poorest people struggle routinely for water, food, decent housing, and decent work. Add to that war, refugees, and a global pandemic.

Years ago, I came across a question. I can't remember who asked it, but it was about global poverty. It could just as easily have been asked about the disappearing species, mass shootings, the opioid epidemic, or the relentless assault on public schools. It could have been about the rise of fascism, racism, or the many other faces of injustice. Here's the question: *What insanity makes us think this is not our problem?* It's true. All of these challenges belong to us. They are ours. We either see their urgency and get to work... or we are truly mad. We are at that critical point where we either push hard enough to pass a better world to our children or we fail them. Fortunately, on this very day, millions of concerned citizens of the world are hard at work saving everything from wolves to voting rights. We are more organized and smarter than ever. But to prevail, we will have to accelerate world change.

In 1959, Martin Luther King, Jr., visited the two-story building in Mumbai (then Bombay) that had served as Mahatma Gandhi's home and headquarters during the struggle for Indian independence. His room has been preserved, and from behind a partition, visitors can see that it's mostly empty but for a sleeping mat, spinning wheels, and a few objects. King went to the building as part of a trip to India to learn more about Gandhian principles. His visit to that room is described in *CounterPunch*[3] by historian Vijay Prashad, director of Tricontinental: Institute for Social Research:

> He was moved by the space where Gandhi sat, now cordoned off from the public. King wanted to go and sit in the room, among Gandhi's remaining objects. The Museum's curator was hesitant, but could not refuse a State guest. King meditated on the floor, where Gandhi once did. Hours went by. The curator asked King's companions when they planned to leave, since he had to close the Bhavan. King asked if he could stay the night, by himself, and sleep where Gandhi had slept. The curator, once more, had to allow his guest this privilege. King did so, to the discomfort of his friends.
>
> The next morning, King wrote in the guest book, "To have the opportunity of sleeping in the house where Gandhiji slept is an experience that I will never forget."

King's bold request took his experience of Gandhi's room to a different level. This same boldness showed up in his dreams for the world and in how he fought for his vision. "I have the audacity to believe that people everywhere can have three meals a day for their bodies, education and culture for their minds, and dignity, equality and freedom for their spirits."

The need today for bold action is stark, and our urgent challenges demand more than half-hearted actions. The meek have never changed the world. While few of us are as bold as Martin Luther King, Jr., we are all called to be more audacious. It took audacity for Doug Tallamy and Michelle Alfandari to launch Homegrown National Park. And it took audacity for my neighbor to place that note on ninety front doors asking us to let our yards look a little messier for the good of tiny critters we seldom think about.

A life's purpose

"The two most important days in your life are the day you are born and the day you find out why."
—Mark Twain

"What do I want to do with my life?" is such a simple question. But it's one many of us struggle to answer. Socrates spent his days like a gadfly challenging citizens in the gathering places of Athens about their tightly held beliefs. He would ask them *Why?* He held that "an unexamined life is not worth living." So, how's your "examination" going? Do you know your purpose? Of course, we all have more than one. A parent's is to raise their children well. For a time, your purpose may be to care for an ailing relative or friend. But, we're talking about something different here: that special calling or vocation. Some people seem to know what that is from birth. Others choose simply to wander, and do so in a wonderful way. But like many, you may be trying to discover a purpose. This search could unfold over the course of months or a lifetime of years. It may be better thought of not as a buried treasure to be found (although that does happen), but rather as a garden to cultivate. What's your dream for your life's work? What gives it meaning? If your monthly expenses were covered, what would you do? How could the world be different, better, because of you?

It's easy to feel stressed out with all the needs in our broken world. So start with this freeing thought: There is no way *you* can save the world. No matter how hard you try it's just not possible. Providing clean water and sanitation to India's 638,000 villages is probably beyond you. And that's just one of ten million needs. So, relax, it's not all up to you. However… you feel the tug to make a difference and want to do more. How do you move from saving "the world" to something a bit more manageable?

When asked how to avoid becoming overwhelmed, theologian Marcus Borg said "It's like being part of a quilter's group. Don't worry about the entire quilt; just focus on your square." Go ahead, breathe that sigh of relief and remember: As we focus on our own square, we can rest assured millions of others are sewing away on their own patches too. And together, we will create a quilt of wholeness and beauty. What's the most important square to work on? Some of us worry that if we choose *this*, we can't do *that*. Not wanting to miss anything, we often put off deciding and end up doing nothing. Inertia is the enemy of change—whether you're making a quilt or making a better world. Instead, imagine as you work on your square that you're at a quilting bee. You're not missing the other squares because while you (and your co-activists) work on your square, others around you are working on theirs. You are listening, sharing with quilters in the larger community, and finding ways to work together, because all good causes are connected. Your patch won't attempt to solve all the problems in the galaxy. But you could, for example, focus on helping your town's mothers with children experiencing homelessness with shelter, counseling, school work, and getting a job. For these struggling moms and kids, you've created the most important square in the world. Is it worth it? If you're clear about your purpose and find meaning pursuing it, you will think less about the cost and more about the rewards, for they can be enormous.

The gift of agency

You could take a walk tomorrow morning or you could sleep in and be late for whatever you had planned. Will you have bacon, eggs, biscuits, and gravy for breakfast? Yogurt and fruit? Ice cream and Brussels sprouts? Or skip it altogether? Agency is our ability to *decide what to do, and then do it.* It's been said that we are masters of our fate, captains of our soul. Within constraints (we can't teleport to Mars, at least not *yet*), we can choose our actions. This is at the heart of world-changing: We can *choose* to make a difference. My friend Gary Gunderson saw this a number of years ago in South Africa. "That's where I learned the language of agency—in the radical disconnection of apartheid, the shattering of families from HIV/AIDS, and the incoherence of apartheid using religion against people," he said. "Even in that setting, people made choices to *move*, to *do*. They worked, healed, resisted. Those are all expressions of agency." It can be an easy default to drift through the days, weeks, years, but we don't have to be bound by our past habits. "Sometimes agency is all you have to work with," Gary told me. "Life may be incoherent; you may be disconnected. But you still can get up in the morning and move. It's a fundamental capacity to choose to move toward life."

Agency is our ability to act on our will. And when you combine agency with habit, you create a whole new power. In *The Power of Habit*, New York Times reporter Charles Duhigg describes how philosopher William James suffered a long bout of self-doubt and depression, including thoughts of suicide.[4] Before taking any drastic step, however, James decided to spend one year believing he controlled his free will, that he could change things. Duhigg continues:

> Later he would famously write that the will to believe is the most important ingredient in creating belief in change. And that one of the most important methods for creating that belief was

habits. Habits, he noted, are what allow us to "do a thing with difficulty the first time, but soon do it more and more easily, and finally, with sufficient practice, do it semi-mechanically, or with hardly any consciousness at all." Once we choose who we want to be, people grow "to the way in which they have been exercised, just as a sheet of paper or a coat, once creased or folded, tends to fall forever afterward into the same identical folds."

If you believe you can change—if you make it a habit—the change becomes real. This is the real power of habit: the insight that your habits are what you choose them to be. Once that choice occurs—and becomes automatic—it's not only real, it starts to seem inevitable, the thing, as James wrote, that bears "us irresistibly toward our destiny, whatever the latter may be."

Yes, our world's messed up. But we can choose to make it better. As we address our chosen cause, our starting point is to take one act, and then another, and another. We learn new things as we go along, we win some, we fail some, and we adjust. So, how much agency does each of us have? Enough.

CHAPTER TWO

Your bold goal

"My goal is simple," said Stephen Hawking. "It is a complete understanding of the universe." Impossible? Of course. But with a less ambitious goal, how far would he have gone? As he reached for the stars (*sorry!*), what they're made of and all things related and unrelated, Hawking stretched our understanding of the universe. Does it matter whether what we're trying to do is ambitious? Absolutely! What we accomplish is directly related to our goals.

In the 1980s, I was part of the mission-oriented Oakhurst Baptist Church in metro-Atlanta. It had recently gone through a transformation. In the 1970s, the all-White neighborhood it sat in was integrating and many of the church members fretted over what would happen if an African-American tried to join. So, the pastor stood in the pulpit one Sunday morning and made it clear that there wasn't going to be a vote—any of God's children would be fully welcomed as members. When the first Blacks joined, most of the Whites quickly left, shrinking the church from more than 1,000 members to around 150. By the time I arrived in 1980, these remaining members and some new ones had leased out some of the larger buildings to the telephone company and retreated to the oldest building. But, by embracing integration, they'd run off the folks who weren't going to do much world-changing and they attracted those who were. The small but mighty Oakhurst congregation spawned a number of missions: a restaurant for people experiencing homelessness, a residential addiction treatment program for unsheltered men (third floor of the church), a local Witness for Peace group, and a sanctuary for Central American refugees. The church housed the regional office of Clergy and Laity Concerned, founded by Martin Luther King, Jr. The Baptist Peace Fellowship was founded there, as was *Seeds*, a national magazine about U.S. and world hunger, where I spent almost a decade. Not too bad for a small congregation.

Oakhurst's approach to mission was borrowed from the Church of the Savior in Washington, D.C. To start something new, a member first had to have a "call" to take on some challenge, such as homelessness, loneliness, world peace. Then a second person had to join in the same calling. Next, they invited others to join them in discovering a way to address the issue. After they had developed their plan, two questions had to be asked before they could move forward: *Is this task impossible? And is it likely to fail?* In order to proceed, the congregation had to agree that the answers to both were *Yes!* Surprised? Oakhurst wasn't interested in taking on anything that wasn't impossible and wasn't likely to fail. By the way, many of the mission attempts bombed. We honored those that didn't work and moved on. Had the Oakhurst do-the-impossible groups waited until they had eliminated all or even most chances of failure, not one of those efforts would have ever taken root. If you're taking on something that's going to change our world, it probably *is* impossible. Nelson Mandela, who spent twenty-seven years of his life in prison before becoming South Africa's president, said "It always seems impossible until it's done."

Build your world

"If this world does not have a place for us then another world must be made."

—Zapatista saying

George R.R. Martin's world in *Game of Thrones* captivated millions with its imaginative geography, languages, cities, attire, customs, and strange creatures. Many novelists tell their stories in familiar settings. But some—particularly science fiction and fantasy writers—have the added task of world-building, constructing an entire fictional reality. Their stories unfold in created settings of a distant planet or a school for witches and wizards. They have to answer a myriad of questions. What are the landscape and the weather like? Where do characters live? What is their daily life like? What do they wear? How do they get from one place to another? What plants, animals, or other creatures live here? Likewise, those of us trying to change the real world should have at least a rough picture of the one we want to create. What does this new world look like? Maybe we can't see it clearly. But we should try. World-building in the real world is tough! Let's say we want to improve health care in a remote Appalachian town. Tolkien could tap a new affordable clinic into existence with his typewriter. We can't. If we want a different world, as the Zapatista saying goes, we'll have to create it the old-fashioned way. But first, we have to imagine it. In her TED animation, *How to Build a Fictional World*,[5] children's book author Kate Messner gives some pointers useful to both writers *and* those of us who want to change our world:

- Start with a place and time so you'll know where you are.

- Create a time-line to show how the world came to be. What events shaped it?

- Draw out details of the world: What rules are in place? Who has power? What does the society value most?

- Ask, how do the inhabitants live? How do they treat one another?

- Ask what technology exists.

Civil rights activists imagined a world where all people were treated equally. Martin Luther King, Jr., was world-building when he said, "I have a dream that my four little children will one day live in a nation where they will not be judged by the color of their skin but by the content of their character." Mahatma Gandhi was great at it. He imagined, against all odds, the British kicked out and an India ruled by Indians. He also imagined and worked for a classless society (a radical idea in a culture rooted in caste), where people of different religions peaceably coexist. Going further, he imagined the ideal village:

> It is a complete republic, independent of its neighbors for its vital wants, and yet interdependent for many other wants in which dependence is a necessity. Thus, every village's first concern will be to grow its own food crops and cotton for its cloth. It should have a reserve for its cattle, recreation and playground for adults and children. Then if there is more land available, it will grow *useful* money crops, thus excluding… tobacco, opium, and the like. The village will maintain a village theater, school and public hall. It will have its own water works ensuring clean water supply. This can be done through controlled wells and tanks. Education will be compulsory up to the final basic course…"[6]

Business management guru Peter Drucker said, "The best way to predict the future is to create it." And the first step to *that* is to imagine it. What's your vision? If your focus is a better food system, think about your world in twenty years. What does the ideal setup look like? Who grows the food, and where and how is it processed and moved to the dinner table? Who owns the food stores? What kinds of warehouses are there and who owns them? What rules make the food safe and healthy, and how did they come about? The visioning part of planning is too often seen as an obligatory activity, a box to check along the way, but imaginative world-building can be powerful. Many successful people, including athletes, entrepreneurs, and entertainers, as well as everyday others, use visualization techniques to help their goals become reality. For them, imagining an outcome increases its odds of happening. The envisioned world draws us toward it because it speaks to both our reason and our aspirations.

A bold, audacious goal

"The tragedy of life doesn't lie in not reaching your goal. The tragedy lies in having no goal to reach. It isn't a calamity to die with dreams unfulfilled, but it is a calamity not to dream. It is not a disgrace not to reach the stars, but it is a disgrace to have no stars to reach for. Not failure, but low aim, is a sin."

—Benjamin Mays

In 2012, President Obama awarded Bill Foege the Medal of Freedom, the nation's highest civilian honor. Foege was not as well-known as some of the others awarded at the White House on that April day—Bob Dylan, Madeleine Albright, John Glenn, Toni Morrison—but he has arguably helped save more lives than any living person. Among other positions, he has directed the CDC, headed The Carter Presidential Center, and has been advising the Gates Foundation on health initiatives. I got to know him when he served on the *Seeds* magazine board of directors. In the early1980s, UNICEF director James Grant approached Foege with a proposition: UNICEF and the World Health Organization may be able to get beyond their turf wars and do more good if a third party, Foege, would chair a Task Force for Child Survival. This campaign would help the world's children on an unprecedented scale. At that time, there were a number of low-cost ways to save millions of children who died each year, but they weren't being deployed on a global scale. Having already led in the remarkable eradication of smallpox, Foege agreed to serve. He was now signing on to an even greater challenge, a Big Hairy Audacious Goal.

In *Built to Last: Successful Habits of Visionary Companies*, authors Jim Collins and Jerry Porras describe their conclusions from six years researching the question: *What makes companies exceptional?* One finding was that most of the visionary companies they examined had a bold mission or "Big Hairy Audacious Goal" (BHAG, pronounced *bee-hag*). They point to the difference between "merely having a goal and becoming committed to a huge, daunting challenge—like a big mountain to climb."[7] It's "clear, compelling, and people 'get it' right away," says Collins in *Good to Great*.[8] "A BHAG serves as a unifying focal point of effort, galvanizing people and creating team spirit as people strive toward a finish line." But there's a difference between a good and a bad BHAG, he says. A bad one is set with bravado while a good one is set with understanding. A good BHAG, he continues, will be found in that intersection between three questions: "What are you deeply passionate about? What can you be best in the world at? What drives your economic engine?" The very same principles apply to doing good and changing the world.

Many explorers had bold goals: Columbus wanted to reach India by sea, Magellan wanted to circumnavigate the world, Lewis and Clark explored the American northwest as they made their way to the Pacific. Audacious engineering goals include the U.S. transcontinental railroad, digging a fifty-mile canal across Panama, and Henry Ford's dream to manufacture an automobile the average person could afford. Sometimes a movement's bold goals culminate in specific legislation: abolishing slavery (1865), gaining women's suffrage (1920), ending child labor (1938 and other years), achieving civil rights (1964), striving for equal pay for equal work (pending). Along with bold goals, of course, come bold failures. All of these examples had them, and so will we all…that is, if we're trying to do something great.

A BHAG realized: the Child Survival Revolution

Back to our story about Bill Foege and his Medal of Freedom for helping change the world… In 1980, fifteen million children under the age of five died each year: forty thousand every day. Yet most of these deaths were preventable. In 1982, a collaboration of groups launched the Child Survival Campaign. Its goal was simple: cut the number of child deaths by half and do it within five to fifteen years using low-cost technologies and new social mobilization practices. Reaching the goal meant seven million children would be saved every year. The campaign focused on four approaches: 1) tracking an infant's monthly weight on a growth chart so the parents know if the baby is not growing properly; 2) oral rehydration therapy, a simple mixture of salt, sugar, and water that can save the life of a child with diarrhea; 3) the promotion of breast feeding; and 4) immunizations against the basic childhood diseases. Over time, the campaign engaged every U.N. agency, every government in the world, faith-based communities, civic clubs (Rotarians donated hundreds of millions of dollars for polio eradication, for example), and virtually every sector of society. It showed what a unified global effort could accomplish.

In 1988, I sat down with UNCIEF chief James Grant in his New York office for *Seeds* to discuss what drove the 1980 idea. "We talked about the possibility for a child survival and development revolution. What we meant by the word *revolution* was not violent turmoil, but dramatic progress within a limited period of years, progress you would normally expect to take much longer," he told me.

"An analogy would be the Green Revolution of the late 1960s and the early 1970s, when a series of countries managed to double their wheat and rice production. This would have taken twenty to forty years to accomplish."

> When we launched the Child Survival Revolution, it was like launching a missile into space. Was it going to take off? And it did. In the first month it received support, beginning with the Secretary-General of the United Nations but also encompassing people as different as Margaret Thatcher, Rajiv Gandhi, and Olaf Palme. This brought us a very satisfying feeling.

> Tremendous satisfaction also came after the initiatives in Colombia, the first country to apply these social mobilization concepts in this form.... Salvadorans discovered that more of their children had died in 1984 from not being immunized than the total killed or injured in the country's war. The society convinced itself that the least it could do is lay down its arms to shoot its children with vaccines three times a year. And they did this in 1985, 1986, 1987, and 1988. This example has been picked up in Lebanon, in Uganda and several other parts of the world.[9]

Grant told me that the immunization launch was the most spectacular he'd seen, "Immunization levels have risen from less than 10 percent in 1980 to well over 50 percent today [1988]." This was a remarkable achievement in just eight years. James Grant died in 1995, so he didn't see his goal fully reached, but he had witnessed the campaign's trajectory. By 1990, the number of child deaths had dropped from fifteen million to twelve million. By 2011, it had dropped below seven million. It took a little longer than visionaries like James Grant and Bill Foege had hoped, but the bold goal of cutting child deaths in half was reached. This is doubly impressive because the global population grew from less than five billion in 1980 to seven billion in 2011: There were more children to protect.

The global effort was successful because people understood and believed in that singular goal. Of course, it was supported by countless sub-goals, and sub-sub-goals. Some may worry that such a singular target will thwart creativity, but it didn't slow down the technical and social innovations needed to save the children; it just focused them. Innovations ramped up as the various hurdles and opportunities appeared. Each country and region had its own unique challenges needing unique solutions, but the power was in the fact that everyone was working toward the same thing: cutting the number of child deaths by half. Reflecting years later on the campaign, Bill Foege said they found from the beginning that "It's important to define, What is success? What's the last mile? When will you know that you've achieved it? Then people sign on for a definite end, rather than signing on because they're interested in a project."[10]

Rallying to do the impossible

After four decades of build-up, by 1980, the United States and the Soviet Union had a combined twenty-five thousand nuclear weapons pointed at each other. Clearly, the world would not survive a nuclear exchange, yet thousands of new weapons were still being stockpiled. A conventional war between the superpowers would almost certainly escalate into a nuclear war. Political scientist and activist Randall Forsberg decided to do something bold. She pushed to reduce the nuclear arsenals to lessen the risk. Her four-page "Call to Halt the Nuclear Arms Race[11]" pointed out that in half an hour a fraction of the weapons could "destroy all the cities in the northern hemisphere." Yet twenty thousand more nuclear warheads were planned. This escalation, she wrote, would "increase hair-trigger readiness for a massive nuclear exchange."

The Nuclear Freeze campaign's goal was bold and simple: Don't build any more nuclear weapons. The effort mobilized people across the nation. Massive public demonstrations of support for the freeze took place around the country, including one in Central Park with as many as one million people. Twelve states and two-hundred seventy-five cities endorsed the effort: 70 percent of Americans supported it. In 1983, Democrats in the House of Representatives passed legislation calling for a freeze and made it part of their party platform in 1984. Similar responses were happening in Europe and elsewhere. That year, hawkish President Reagan suggested his openness to nuclear abolition. The global massive outcry became a leading factor that led Presidents Reagan and Gorbachev to agree to begin to reduce nuclear arsenals in 1986. The out-of-control proliferation of weapons was slowed by a simple, clarion call. Behind great accomplishments are people who deliberately and persistently pursue a singular big goal.

Aligning around a focal point

An effort aligned with an ambitious goal can accomplish the impossible. In 1961, President Kennedy announced a goal of sending astronauts to the moon. "We choose to go to the Moon in this decade and do the other things, not because they are easy, but because they are hard… because that challenge is one that we are willing to accept, one we are unwilling to postpone, and one we intend to win." Space stations have orbited Earth since the seventies, so we've gotten used to people being out there. But in 1961, a moon trip was a dizzying notion. NASA would have to be transformed, infrastructure would have to be built, 400,000 people would have to be engaged, and (in today's dollars) $100 billion would be spent.[12] Thousands of problems would have to be solved. The effort would, in Kennedy's words, "organize and measure the best of our energies and skills." Eight years later, the world watched in awe as Neil Armstrong stepped onto the moon's surface. Ambitious goal achieved. Check.

Long before a step-by-step plan, a goal's superpower is its ability to focus and align thoughts and actions over time. Without a goal, even good organizations with talented leaders and staff are doomed to wander in the land of mediocrity. They may be doing good work but a great opportunity is lost. Having an audacious goal doesn't mean you'll know *how* you'll reach it. No one in 1961 knew how to send people to the moon. It's a statement of intent, an organizing point. Everyone is focused, asking, "How do I help us get there? What must we do next?"

To launch your bold goal, consider the following:

- **It will take a village to reach.** The nonprofit KaBOOM builds playgrounds with community participation. To reach their goal of placing a playground "within walking distance of every child in America," they will have to join with all kinds of local partners. Engaging the help of many people for a bold cause can increase your odds of success.

- **It has to be believable.** A goal focuses your energy on a vision, as well as you can imagine it, of what you want the future to be. It can *look* impossible, but it's *got* to be achievable. Bill Foege, who has spent a lifetime pursuing bold global health goals, said that an important ingredient of eradicating smallpox "was simply the belief that it could be done. In fact, in retrospect, the belief that it could be done seems like the most important factor in the global eradication effort."

- **Your ambitious goal is part of a historic continuum.** Malala Yousafzai struggles for the right of children to have education. For that effort, she is the youngest person to receive the Nobel Peace Prize. Her goal is to ensure that every girl in the world has access to twelve years of free, safe, quality primary and secondary education by 2030. She didn't invent the priority of educating girls. In fact, she benefitted from others who sought to make sure she had an education.

Our goals build on decades of accomplishments of those who have gone before us.

- **Your goal is connected to other goals.** Even if the scope of your bold goal isn't global, it will likely contribute to other greater goals. Citizens in the Indian state of Uttar Pradesh recently set a world record of planting almost fifty million trees in twenty-four hours. This effort was part of India's larger goal of increasing its forested land from 192 million acres to 235 million acres by 2030. And that goal is one more step toward an even greater goal of restoring more than 800 million acres of forests worldwide. A number of groups are now calling for the planting of one trillion trees (there are about three trillion trees on earth today).[13] This could be nested in an even larger goal of fighting climate change, and so on. It's all part of the ultimate Big Hairy Audacious Goal of saving humanity's ability to live on the planet—as soon as possible!

- **Your goal can be about filling in gaps.** The Y2Y vision is a two thousand-mile interconnected system of wildlands and waterways that will stretch from Canada's Yukon to Montana's Yellowstone National Park to ensure the survival of animals such as caribou and grizzly bears. The East Coast Greenway is a three thousand-mile off-road bike trail from Maine to Key West, Florida. Both efforts are literally about filling in gaps in our landscape from point to point. And both find local partners to help fill in those local gaps. While not always so literal, the giant gap between where you are presently and your ambitious goal can be broken down into many smaller gaps. Each one will be filled in through persistence and creative energy.

- **Reaching the goal will be messy.** No great accomplishment was achieved without stumbles. Some worse than others. Many people died building the Panama Canal, trying to sail around the world (including Magellan himself), and freeing India from British colonial rule. There's no easy, smooth path. You hit dead-ends and have to back up and try another way. There are never enough resources. Shortcuts, mistakes, and sometimes even disasters occur along the way. Do what you think is best at the time. At the very least, you'll learn something to help you take another step.

- **Ambitious goals transform.** An organization committed to doing something great will never be the same. It will be stretched and reinvented. Your goal may be local, like making sure all veterans in your city have housing, bringing a dying neighborhood back to life, or radically increasing high school graduation rates. You may not send someone to the moon, but as you strive to reach your bold goal the lives of those involved will be transformed.

Half Earth: an ambitious goal to save the planet

"I am convinced that only by setting aside half the planet in reserve, or more, can we save the living part of the environment and achieve the stabilization required for our own survival."

—E.O. Wilson

Scientists measure Earth's 4.5 billion years in eras and epochs. Humans have been around for only two hundred thousand years and civilization for about six thousand. To put that in perspective, if the history of Earth were compressed into one year, humans don't show up until after five o'clock on the evening of December 31, civilization begins just one minute before midnight, and Leonardo Da Vinci is painting the Mona Lisa just twenty seconds before the year ends.[14] The Holocene epoch began 11,000 years ago with the end of the last ice age. Today scientists increasingly agree that we have begun to wreak enough havoc on our home planet to warrant a new geologic age, *Anthropocene*. It began somewhere between the industrial revolution and the first atom bomb, when humans began to impact the atmosphere, geology, hydrology, and ecosystems of the earth enough to alter its natural cycles. In this fleeting moment, we have halved the number of trees and changed about half of the earth's surface. Signs of the Anthropocene include the shrinking polar ice sheets; rising seas; climate disruption; the loss of tropical forests; acidification of oceans; the sharp rises of CO_2, methane, and other gasses; and climbing global temperatures.

The most sobering sign is the massive extinction of plant and animal species due to ecosystem disruptions—and the growing possibility of our own demise. And the rate of extinction is accelerating. There are roughly eight million species (including microorganisms) on the planet. In 2019, the Intergovernmental Science-Policy Platform on Biodiversity and Ecosystem Services reported[15] that about one million of them are threatened with extinction, "more than ever before in human history." What is causing this mass extinction? A commonly used acronym HIPPO lists the human actions in order of importance: Habitat destruction; Invasive species; Pollution; Population growth; and Overhunting (and Overfishing). In his book *Half-Earth*, biologist E.O. Wilson cites a major survey that found that one-fifth of the roughly twenty-five thousand mammals, birds, reptiles, and amphibians are threatened with extinction. But it's not all bad news: Many of these are being stabilized through conservation efforts. He points out that "while 22 species had slipped into extinction, 227 had been saved that would likely have otherwise disappeared." For example, conservation efforts have cut by half the extinction of bird species, and saved such animals as green sea turtles and bighorn sheep. However:

The declining world of biodiversity cannot be saved by the piecemeal operations in current use alone. It will certainly be mostly lost if conservation continues to be treated as a luxury item in national budgets. The extinction rate our behavior is now imposing on the rest of life, and seems destined to continue, is more correctly viewed as the equivalent of a Chicxulub-sized asteroid strike played out over several human generations.[16]

Of course, reality doesn't give a damn whether some people pretend this isn't happening! Wilson says that the Earth with its complex and interdependent ecosystem is rapidly losing ground...literally. "The only hope for the species still living is a human effort commensurate with the magnitude of the problem," he says. Fortunately, Wilson points out, every country has some kind of "protected-area system." But, combined, they only safeguard approximately 15 percent of the land mass and just 3 percent of the oceans. It's nowhere near enough. The biodiversity crisis won't be solved with postage stamp-sized nature reserves hemmed in on all sides by our bad practices. Wilson proposes: "Only by committing half of the planet's surface to nature can we hope to save the immensity of life-forms that compose it." This is a Big Hairy Audacious Goal for all times: Set aside half of the planet—half the water and half the land—as wilderness to stabilize the threatened species. If he is right, in one future we continue foolishly down the path of habitat destruction and mass extinction, in another future we do something radically different.

Wilson's book is short on exactly how to go about doing this. But so was President Kennedy's announcement of landing on the moon within a decade. Remember, we don't have to worry about The How; to start, we only have to focus on The What, the believable goal. Case in point: Thousands of groups around the planet are already contributing to Wilson's Half-Earth solution. They are taking on the questions, *Is it realistic?, Is it possible?* And they are creating answers. Of course, these questions are eclipsed by *What happens if we don't?*

CHAPTER THREE

New ideas and their spread

All human advances begin as ideas. Ideas like language, the bow and arrow, weaving, and writing emerged slowly over thousands of years and are still evolving. But occasionally we see sudden breakthroughs. The solutions to our challenges also start with ideas. So where do good ideas come from?

Steal and share

Isaac Newton said, "If I have seen further it is by standing on the shoulders of giants." A great quote, but actually he borrowed that metaphor about borrowing from twelfth-century Bernard of Chartres: "We are like dwarfs on the shoulders of giants, so that we can see more than they, and things at a greater distance, not by virtue of any sharpness of sight on our part, or any physical distinction, but because we are carried high and raised up by their giant size." If your group is a nonprofit, or sends direct mail for support, or has a Facebook page, you're already in the borrowing and stealing business. You invented none of those. Martin Luther King, Jr., didn't coin the phrase "beloved community," nor the idea that the arc of the moral universe bends toward justice. Others before him did. The point isn't to do something unique; it's to address a challenge. Artist and social activist Ben Shahn was once asked by a student for advice on which art school to go to. He responded that "a good art school is one that has a good art museum you have to pass by to get to."[17] Just as an art student needs to see great art, we all need to continually expose ourselves to the best ideas and practices—so we'll know which ones to steal!

As you borrow, you're re-combining other peoples' ideas into a new context, making something new. (Naturally you want to stay on the right sides of the legal and ethical lines. Borrowing your neighbor's car without permission could get you in trouble.) Starbucks founder Howard Schultz came up with his coffee experience and culture from the espresso bars of Milan. You may not have to travel far: One of the best places to steal ideas is from your own organization. In 1933, the national Girl Scouts borrowed the idea of selling cookies from its Mistletoe Troop in Muskogee, Oklahoma. If you borrow and steal well, others will borrow and steal your ideas, too. That's how it works.

Cookies, crayons, toys—as toddlers we're taught to share. It's tough at first, but we learn. A big part of playing well with others—and getting things done—is to share ideas freely! "He who receives an idea from me, receives instruction himself without lessening mine; as he who lights his taper at mine, receives light without darkening me," said Thomas Jefferson. "That ideas should freely spread from one to another over the globe, for the moral and mutual instruction of man, and improvement of his condition, seems to have been peculiarly and benevolently designed by nature." Jefferson's friend Benjamin Franklin was also great at sharing. He invented or improved everything from lightning rods and bifocals to swim fins and the flexible catheter. But he patented nothing, insisting that "as we benefit from the inventions of others, we should be glad to share our own... freely and gladly." As polio ravaged the world in the first half of the twentieth century, tens of thousands fell victim each year in the United States alone. In the 1950s, fear of polio was second only to fear of the atom bomb. When Jonas Salk announced his successful polio vaccine, he was an instant hero and considered a miracle worker. Remarkably, he refused to patent the vaccine and forfeited the equivalence today of $7 billion.[18] In sharing his life's work, Salk looked beyond the annual return to the millions whose lives could be protected.

But there's more involved than generosity. Shared ideas are more likely to become reality. "I leave ideas lying around like pencils," said Margaret Mead. "I *want* them to be stolen!"[19] In *Making Ideas Happen*, Behance Founder and CEO Scott Belsky says that the "notion of 'sharing ideas liberally' defies the natural instinct to keep your ideas a secret."

> Yet, among the hundreds of successful creatives I've interviewed, a fearless approach to sharing ideas is one of the most common attributes. Why? Because having the idea is just a tiny step along the road to making that idea happen. During the journey, communal forces are instrumental in refining the very substance of the idea, holding us accountable for making it happen, building the network that will push us to go above and beyond, providing us with valuable material and emotional support, and spreading the word to attract resources and publicity. By sharing your idea, you take the first step in creating the community that will act as a catalyst to making it happen.[20]

WordPress and others have made creating a blog or website easy and more or less free, meaning almost anyone can share ideas planet-wide. But sharing our precious, more tightly-held ideas may still take a mind shift. In *Momentum: Igniting Social Change in the Connected Age*, technology and leadership strategist Allison Fine says we need to move from proprietary to participatory. "Traditional activist organizations tend to work in silos and in isolation from their sister organizations," she says. "These proprietary organizations keep information they consider vital to their survival, like strategic plans and membership lists, tightly sealed. They falsely believe that this information alone equals power."[21] The social sector, says Fine, has been slow to adopt the open-source approach found in programming code.

Hatching ideas

Ideas come to us in conversations, as we're reading, or taking a shower, or even dreaming. We've all had countless thousands of ideas. Occasionally one turns out to be good. But if you need ideas to change your patch of the world, you may not have time to wait for the muse. You may need to force idea generation. You can shake ideas loose through simple brainstorming and other idea-creation processes. In one day of such exercises, a group of Heifer International staff generated 270 marketing ideas to help us find the "next big thing," as well as ways to incrementally improve existing programs. Ideas from that day included a Ground Hog Day campaign, having a balloon in Macy's Thanksgiving Parade, and selling manure patties. While we did none of those things, several of our nuggets moved us forward. Every once in a while, it helps to stop everything and suspend normalcy to crazy-make ideas. A spider lays an egg sac with between a couple hundred and a couple thousand eggs with the hope that some hatchlings will survive to adulthood. That's how many ideas you may need, coming from all sorts of places, so that the few best are able to mature. And as you nurture your better ones, they'll generate yet more good ideas.

We're told not to reinvent the wheel, and that usually makes sense. If you can find a model that helps you address your challenge, borrow it and adjust it to your needs. But sometimes you have to start from scratch. In Portland, Maine, Katherine Freund reinvented the wheel by reinventing who was *behind* the wheel. In 1988, Freund found herself traveling down an unexpected path after an eighty-four-year-old driver who should not have been behind the wheel hit her three-year old son. The boy survived the life-threatening brain injury and is now a healthy adult. But the event led Freund, then working on graduate studies in public policy, to explore this question: What options do seniors have as they lose their ability to drive? It's said that when "I" is replaced with "we," illness becomes wellness. This will certainly matter to the tsunami of elderly people (about ten thousand Americans celebrate their seventieth birthday each day) who need help getting around. In the United States, seniors typically outlive their ability to drive: seven years for men and a decade for women. This impacts their health, as roughly 3.6 million Americans miss or delay medical appointments because they don't have a way to get to them.[22]

Freund's studies after her son's accident ultimately led her to found Independent Transportation Network (ITN), which gave its first ride in 1995 in Portland. For seniors not comfortable driving, especially at night, or who can no longer drive, such a trip can be a lifeline. Residents can schedule trips twenty-four hours a day to get to medical appointments, go grocery shopping, attend religious services, or travel almost anywhere. Volunteer drivers even come to the door to help the passenger into and out of the car. Today, the nonprofit ITN affiliates in communities in a dozen states, from San Diego to Boston, to offer volunteer-based transportation in personal cars, providing more than a million rides to older and vision-impaired people. While no cash changes hands at the time of the ride, ITN created several ways to pay. Families can put money into senior accounts, seniors can donate their cars for ride credits, and a volunteer driver can donate miles to others. Yes, use the wheels that already exist. And by the way, do you need a better one?

A better way

Most services in our communities began when people turned a good idea into reality. Those that work spread to other places. One such model called *Housing First* or *Permanent Supportive Housing* has been spreading to city after city. In the early 1980s during the Reagan administration, a homelessness epidemic suddenly hit a scale not seen since the Great Depression. Many thought the problem was temporary and could be addressed with night shelters and soup kitchens. As government support waned, energy emerged from faith communities and local groups. But the problem didn't go away, and in the following decades the challenge of homelessness has seemed intractable. But a few people began looking at it differently.

Like Tanya Tull. She catches things others miss and then creates solutions based on what she sees. She has not only founded five nonprofits, but she also helped start the "housing first" movement. While in her early twenties—and after three months of receiving welfare herself—Tull became a social worker in the Skid Row area of Los Angeles. After a while she left that to pursue other activities. In 1979, she read an article about hundreds of children living in the same Skid Row hotels she had known a decade earlier. She shifted her attention to found "Para Los Niños" to help those children. Later she founded a housing organization in the area. And in 1988, she started "A Community of Friends" to create affordable housing in partnership with mental health agencies that provided services to the residents. Seeing that shelters were not the long-term answer, Tull later founded Beyond Shelter to help families experiencing homelessness to find permanent housing. The idea was to place families in homes and then provide the supportive services they needed to become self-sufficient. Beyond Shelter has gone on to develop affordable housing in low-income neighborhoods, along with support services for the residents. Tull's approach is credited with helping thousands of families in Los Angeles County get permanent housing, and her institute has trained more than a thousand people in the housing first model.

Around this time and across the country, Sam Tsemberis wondered about the homeless people he passed as he walked to work at Belleview Hospital in New York City. Over time, he became so intrigued by what he saw that he left Bellevue to become a street outreach worker. He knew the system for dealing with chronically homeless people was broken. Before they could be rewarded with housing, people first had to deal with their addictions, mental illness, and other challenges. This simply didn't work. Tsemberis watched the never-ending stream cycling from the street to treatment programs and hospitals and then back to the street. In 1992, he gathered a small group to listen to the people they served. This led them to an approach similar to the one discovered by Tanya Tull: Get the person into safe housing and then work with them on other issues. "We began taking people from the streets into an apartment of their own... nothing fancy but the privacy and dignity of being able to live not in a crowded shelter setting," he told a TEDx audience.[23] "There, they could cook and eat what they wanted, watch television, do what they wanted. Have dignity." Their approach had two parts: First, the group helped people find an apartment (with a rental stipend allowing the person to pay a landlord). Then they offered wraparound service teams who would visit residents in their homes to observe and help them avoid going from one agency after another. "It seems, in hindsight, so simple that somebody who had to walk to the church program to get breakfast and then find a place where they could use the bathroom during the day and then walk another two miles to go to the shelter at night would do so much better in an apartment where the kitchen, bathroom and bedroom were all in one place," said Tsemberis. "They had those survival skills all along, they just weren't as evident to us." As the early results began to be known, others tried the controversial model.

Over time, studies began to discover another benefit. A chronically homeless person typically costs a community around $40,000 a year (jail time, emergency room visits, social services). With housing first, that drops to $16,000 a year. Besides saving taxpayer money, the approach opens up the capacity of over-stretched shelters, feeding programs, and other services. Terrence McCoy reported in the *Washington Post* that "the federal government tested the model on 734 homeless across 11 cities, finding the model dramatically reduced levels of addiction, as well as shrunk health-related costs by half. 'Adults who have experienced chronic homelessness may be successfully housed and can maintain their housing,' the report declared." McCoy says that Tsemberis "unfurled a model so simple children could grasp it, so cost-effective fiscal hawks loved it, so socially progressive liberals praised it."[24] Today, Tsemberis leads Pathways to Housing, the organization he founded in 1993. The group boasts that after three years, "85 percent of those people are still in their apartments."[25] This model has been copied in more than forty U.S. cities and internationally, as well. How do you create a better solution? As with Tull and Tsemberis, most new models are the result of years of work. They emerge from the stew of information, data, listening, experience, intuition, and creativity.

Change doesn't always happen easily. Don't expect your great innovation to be loved at first sight. In *Ignore Everybody*, artist Hugh Macleod says that good ideas have lonely childhoods. "Creating an idea or brand that fights the Powers That Be can be a lot of fun, and very rewarding. The bad news is that they're called the Powers That Be for a reason," he said. "Most team members in any industry are far more concerned with the power relationships inside their immediate professional circle than what may actually be interesting and useful for the customer."[26] Sadly, a great idea can also set off a toxic chemical reaction from naysayers who feel threatened that the idea's success could somehow upset their world. Hopefully, the good idea has enough momentum from its own logic and enough champions to push past the worriers and saboteurs. Hopefully, the organization has leaders who protect and encourage good idea- making. Once the idea survives its lonely childhood, it can flourish and help create a place where the next idea will not be quite so alone. So, be on the lookout for the good idea and when you meet it, befriend it. Become its champion!

The spread of ideas

Inspired by frequent electricity blackouts, in 2002 Brazilian mechanic Alfredo Moser thought up a simple technology—literally a brilliant idea for people with no electricity. Just fill a clear plastic soda bottle with water (add bleach to prevent algae clouding), cut a hole in the roof of the house and snugly place the bottle in the hole, partly above and partly below the roof, and seal it to keep the rain out. It takes less than an hour to make and install. The sunlight will brighten the room as though it were a 50-watt bulb. Of course, it shines only during the day. Moser's lights slowly spread until 2011, when news features and viral videos swept the solar bulbs through cyberspace, including instructions on making the lights. The lights were being adopted around the world. One group in the Philippines was installing 140,000 lights in slums across the country. Today these simple bulbs bring light to once dark rooms for millions from Ecuador to India, and entrepreneurs have created solar bulb-making and installation businesses. What's more wasteful than a great solution that doesn't spread? And what's more powerful than the expansion of a practice that improves life? But how do good ideas spread? How does an improvement—a brand new idea or great tweak on an existing one—travel from place to place and go to scale? Being part of the world-change tribe means having the trust and the generosity to share deeply—not just the nuts and bolts of a practice, but also the deeper nuances of why a practice works.

Stakeholder Health is an informal group I work with that's comprised mostly of healthcare system leaders who have both smarts and hearts. Spread across the country, they have this in common: getting their hospitals outside their walls to help vulnerable people in their communities have better health. From the outset, the Stakeholder community shied away from the idea that their practices could be "replicated." Actually, these practices (health asset mapping, navigation networks, data-driven "hotspotting" of where high-need patients live) have to be *adapted* as they move from one place to another. That's because hospitals are found in a *place*, and each place has unique challenges and assets. When the Memphis model of connecting congregations with hospitals was tried in North Carolina, significant changes had to be made. The health systems were different, and so were the internal champions, the external partners, the demographics, the culture, and the politics. The North Carolina adaptation has thrived and developed a few of its own innovations.

Most complex practices can't be replicated, they refuse to mechanically "plug and play" in a new setting. But they *can* be borrowed and adapted. How do we boost the chances that proven solutions will spread? We share, sometimes deeply, things that work and hopes for the next phase through stories, site visits, data-filled PowerPoints, blog posts, in conversations over lunch, or on the phone. Good practices evolve as they migrate. If we stay connected to early adopters, we'll see what changes they make and learn new ways to improve our own practice. As a practice spreads, it creates momentum for large-scale change. How do ideas like the solar bottle lights spread? Psychologist Nico van Oudenhoven and sociologist Rekha Wazir described[27] five different paths for replicating social programs in a paper for UNESCO. Here's my summary of their paths:

- **Franchise Approach.** With a central agency that provides "technical assistance, marketing, training and other services in a cookie-cutter" way. The rules are fixed, can't be changed.

- **Mandated Replication.** Program is mandated top-down, usually from a government. No choice in how the program works.

- **Staged Replication.** Three stages: 1) Pilot, the concept is tested; 2) Demonstration, the program is tried in a variety of settings; and 3) Rollout, go to scale.

- **Concept Replication.** Focus is on not the specifics of the prototype program but on the components and principles that made it work. These are then adapted to fit the local context.

- **Spontaneous Replication.** Program spreads spontaneously through informal contacts. Communication is "a two-way process of convergence where participants 'create and share information.'"

A viral idea for our hopes and dreams

In 2011, artist Candy Chang used her creative powers to connect her post-Hurricane Katrina New Orleans neighbors to their own dreams and to each other. Dealing with depression related to the unexpected death of a loved one caused Chang to reflect on what really matters in life. She turned the side of an abandoned house in her neighborhood into a giant chalkboard. She stenciled it with the sentence, "Before I die, I want to _____." Passersby were provided chalk and invited to fill in the blanks. Surprisingly, in one day, they had filled the entire wall with specific hopes, aspirations, dreams. She described what happened next on her website:

> By the next day, the wall was full of responses and it kept growing: Before I die I want to... sing for millions, plant a tree, hold her one more time, straddle the International Date Line, see my

daughter graduate, eat more everything, abandon all insecurities, be completely myself… She understood her neighbors in new and enlightening ways, and the wall reminded her that she's not alone as she tries to make sense of her life.[28]

"This neglected space became a constructive one," Chang told a TED-talk audience.[29] "And people's hopes and dreams made me laugh out loud, tear up, and they consoled me during my own tough times." She asked, "How can we share more of our hopes for our vacant storefronts so our communities can reflect our needs and dreams today?" Later in 2011, a student at the Clinton School of Public Service saw the wall and brought the idea from New Orleans to Little Rock, where at that time the mostly-abandoned Main Street cried out for a bit of human connection. A small group converted the corner of an empty building into a "Before I Die" chalkboard. It was an instant hit. I watched as business women, people who were homeless, lost tourists, and others walked by and momentarily found themselves thinking: What is something I'd like to do in my life? What's important, what's fun, what's an adventure? Some people, myself included, wrote that they wanted to see this abandoned building come to life again. Not too much later the block began to be renovated with a $20 million re-do and other projects began nearby.

Curious about how social change ideas spread, Nicole Dubbs and Kerry Anne McGeary explored with creative people and experts "what it takes to spread ideas that others adopt, adapt, integrate, and ultimately take up as their own." They share four conclusions in the *Stanford Social Innovation Review*:

- Where you intervene in a system is important.

- Stakeholders don't act on abstract ideas.

- Moving away from a traditional program focus is useful.

- Shape the rhetoric and shift action.

Candy Chang was making good use of her degrees in graphic design, architecture, and urban planning. Her chalkboards were helping individuals and communities dream out loud. Shortly after Chang posted a few photos of her New Orleans wall, she began receiving messages from people around the world who wanted to create one in their city. Chang and a few colleagues made it easier for them by creating a website with an online toolkit that advised how to choose a site, get permission, spread the word, and make and maintain the wall. The "build your own wall" section includes stencils, measurements, and detailed information on what materials to use. Mostly through social media, interest in the wall quickly spread. In just a few years, a thousand have been created in seventy countries and in thirty-five languages.

This didn't catch on because of a marketing program and a big budget. It caught on because it was a powerful idea. People saw the images, read the stories, and shared them on social media. Like the Little Rock student, some saw walls as they were traveling and brought the idea home. It also spread because Chang and others saw the interest and created the DIY tools to make it easy to copy. They didn't try to own it, they shared it. What began as one creative woman's outlet to deal with grief grew into a global art project and message board that connects a wild array of aspirations. Chang said that through efforts like the walls, it's important that we keep the perspective that "Life is brief and tender... Thinking about death clarifies your life. Our shared spaces can better reflect what matters to us as individuals and as a community." Here are few things people would like to do before they die: Grow squash, see my dad, own a dog, perform on Broadway, see the woman my daughter grows up to be, finish crocheting my afghan, hug a redwood, visit Paris, learn to play the fiddle, end bullying, fall in love, drive an ice cream truck, and change the world.

Franchise your ideas?

In the 1850s, an ambitious young man named Isaac Singer had developed some improvements to the sewing machine. Needing funds to develop manufacturing distribution capacity, he offered to train people to spread the sales of the Singer sewing machine. This became the first franchise in the United States. Others, such as Coca-Cola bottling, soon followed. One hundred years after Singer, Ray Kroc pioneered fast food franchising with McDonald's. Franchises proved to be an efficient way to spread a business that works in one place to all the other places it should also work. In franchising, the original owner, the *franchisor,* licenses to a *franchisee* the right to use the name and certain elements of an already successful business, such as procedures, training, help in site selection, marketing, and the ability to plug into a product distribution network. The franchisee gets to own a local site of a business with its brand, operational rules, and customer base, and avoids some of the risk of starting from scratch. The franchisor collects fees and the brand spreads at little cost. Today, franchises of all kinds—from fitness centers to tool rentals to coffee shops—make up over $1 trillion a year of the U.S. economy. But franchises can be about more than profits.

One day in 1967, John van Hengel saw a mother of ten rummaging for food behind a Phoenix, Arizona grocery store. Wanting to help people like her, he found a way to get to hungry people the food that could no longer be sold. In doing this, he started St. Mary's, the world's first food bank. The model he created worked and others copied it. A decade later, food banks had spread to eighteen cities. They proliferated in the 1980s in response to the need created by deep cuts in the social safety net. Today, the largest network, Chicago-based Feeding America, serves 46 million people a year through food banks in more than two hundred cities and is affiliated with tens of thousands of food pantries and other feeding programs. This network spread across the country in the 1980s in response to an emergency: People couldn't afford food. It created an infrastructure to better deliver the leftovers of a food industry. They also engage in advocating for government programs for hungry citizens.

Habitat for Humanity is best known for building and rehabbing houses. It's made up of more than fourteen hundred local U.S. affiliates, plus organizations in seventy countries. "Each affiliate coordinates all aspects of Habitat home-building in its local area—fundraising; building site selection; partner family selection and support; house construction; and mortgage servicing," says Habitat's website. Each one also tithes 10 percent of their funds, amounting to millions of dollars, to the work of Habitat overseas. Its fifty-nine-page handbook for U.S. affiliates covers everything from house pricing to logo use. As in franchises, the local affiliate gets the credibility and brand of Habitat International. The practices have been tested in more than a thousand locations, and include training and other benefits.

Like food banks (or libraries, dog parks, or hospitals), many community institutions we now take for granted started somewhere as an idea: a response to a need that became a physical reality. And because they solved a need in one community, they soon spread. If a public library made sense in Benjamin Franklin's Philadelphia, it would make sense in Savannah. Same with fire departments and farmers' markets. Copy initiatives in other places when they make sense in yours. If you see a great idea while traveling and wonder why you don't have one in your town, you may be on to your next project.

CHAPTER FOUR

Step by step

"The secret of getting ahead is getting started. The secret of getting started is breaking your complex overwhelming tasks into small manageable tasks, and then starting on the first one."

—Mark Twain

You may have watched leaders who knew where they were headed and led their teams to achieve amazing results—but never had a plan. They followed their instincts and smarts. Herb Keller, founder of Southwest Airlines, said, "We have a strategic plan, it's called doing things." While there's truth in his emphasis on action, in reality, Southwest Airlines followed many successful strategies; for example, focusing on smaller airports (with less competition) in large urban markets. As critical a plan is to success, it's puzzling how many organizations don't have one. And a plan begins with the goal. In *Managing the Nonprofit Organization*, Peter Drucker describes the importance of the long-range goal:

> If you focus on short-term results, [the team] will all jump in different directions. You'll have a flea circus—as I discovered during my own dismal failure some forty years ago as an executive in an

academic institution. My own thinking has always been long term. But I thought I'd win friends and influence people by giving them some short-term goodies. What I learned was that unless you integrate the vision of all constituencies into the long-range goal, you will soon lose support, lose credibility, and lose respect.

After I'd been beaten to a pulp, I began to look at non-profit executives who did successfully what I had unsuccessfully tried to do. I soon learned that they start out by defining the fundamental change that the non-profit institution wants to make in society and in human beings; then they project that goal onto the concerns of the institution's constituencies.

What fundamental change does your group want to make? A plan will help you name it. Actions with no goal can keep everyone busy, but you'll miss the big opportunities. Once you've determined where you want to boldly go, you'll need to create a map for the journey. Your plan will describe the strategies and actions needed to move the effort from where you currently are to where you aspire to be. The effort is broken into manageable tasks to be carried out by different people. To succeed, the process needs to be participatory without becoming unwieldy, because the power of a plan is gathering the stakeholders, debating the main goal and strategies, getting on the same page, and understanding the importance of where you're actually going together over the next few years. A solid plan identifies the top few priorities for the coming period. It will explain why they were chosen and how they will move the organization toward its main goal.

SMART goals

As the top few priorities are set and energy and resources are focused, the organization is more poised to reach the bold goal. It helps to break down the priorities into sub-goals, strategies, steps, and so on. Many groups use "SMART goals," an approach first articulated in 1981 by management consultant George Doran. They have morphed over the years, but here's a summary:

- **Specific:** Avoid abstract goals. What is it you're trying to accomplish? It can't be fuzzy. Will you know when you hit it?

- **Measurable:** The plan will include ways to measure progress towards each objective and explain how efforts are monitored.

- **Achievable:** Bringing peace to the entire world may be a bit beyond our ability. So, what's something, even with a stretch, you could actually achieve?

- **Realistic:** Be honest about each goal and how it's to be accomplished.

- **Time-bound:** Create time-linked expectations. It's been said that a goal is a dream with a deadline. "Someday" means never. But, with "by the end of next year," you can get there.

Break your goal into doable steps. What does the path to your bold goal look like? Can you map it out? What are the milestones? Every goal or project can be segmented into action steps. In the end you'll have a lot of *action steps*. Each one should start with a verb: *write* the lessons, *research* solutions others use, *convene* key participants, *deliver* the service. Each step must be attached to a specific person, have a deadline, and be SMART.

The idea is to combine a bold goal with SMART goals. For example, to mark the 150th anniversary of Arbor Day, the Arbor Day Foundation launched a Time for Trees initiative with a *specific* goal that was also a stretch: to plant 100 million trees between 2019 and 2022.[30] The goal was *measured* by counting the trees planted—pretty straightforward. While the goal is a stretch (it took the foundation forty-five years to plant its first 300 million trees and now they want to plant another 100 million in less than four years) it is still *achievable*. And it's *realistic*, in part, because the group has a sub-goal to "inspire 5 million tree planters to join the movement by 2022," and has lined up corporate partners for funding and other support. And none of this operation is new; the foundation has been at it since 1972. It is *time-bound* because they hope to have all 100 million trees in the ground by Arbor Day 2022. And, yes, they did meet their goals—100 million trees planted and 5 million people planting them—a whole year early!

While the best way to miss opportunities is to have no plan to follow, the second way is to follow your plan without being flexible. Things change and goals aren't etched in stone. Here's Homegrown National Park's original goal: "20 million acres of native plantings in the U.S. This represents approximately half of the green lawns of privately-owned properties." Now more accurate information enlarges residential neighborhood landscapes from 40 million acres to 46 million. But more important, the earth is currently undergoing its sixth mass extinction—this time due to human activity. "So 20 million acres of lawn is just a tiny fraction of what we need to do," says Doug Tallamy. Our parks and preserves are not enough. "It goes way beyond reducing your lawn. How does a corn farmer in Iowa or a woodlot owner in Pennsylvania join Homegrown National Park?" asks Tallamy. So the new, more audacious goal has expanded from half of the residential lawns to half of all non-government owned property.

A relentless bias toward action

Whether you're taking on a new project or embarking on a new life journey, it all begins with clarity about what you want to accomplish and why. You have your vision, your goal—or at least a glimpse of it. It's been said, "A ship in a harbor is safe, but that is not what ships are for." Getting started means moving from that safe place of an idea to an action in the real world. At some point you hoist the sails and head out to open waters. You may want to raise a million dollars, start an organization, get a degree, or protect a fragile piece of the environment. You know what you want to accomplish and have planned how to get there as well as you can. Remember, you'll never be completely ready, and your first steps won't be perfect—neither will most of the thousands of steps along the way. Knowing this, you can start anyway. Do you have to have a full plan to get started? It's great to have thought out your goal and planned it all out, *but…* some people just start. They plant the first tree, hold up a protest sign, set out that first recycling bin. There's no Big Hairy Audacious Goal, no plan, just a desire to do something. And that's okay, maybe it's great. Young Beethoven didn't start playing the keyboard with a goal of writing nine symphonies. Clara Barton didn't tend to the U.S. Civil War's sick and wounded in order to start the American Red Cross. Gandhi didn't start law school in order to lead India to independence. "How wonderful it is that no one has to wait, but can start right now to gradually change the world!" said Anne Frank, Jewish Holocaust victim and author of *Diary of a Young Girl.* "How wonderful it is that everyone, great and small, can immediately help bring about justice by giving of themselves!" Causes often start with a fuzzy goal and no formal plan. Someone just gets out there and does things. They see what works and what doesn't and adapt as they move forward.

Whether you start with a full-blown plan or just jump in, you can't wait until you have all the answers. "Take the first step in faith," advised Martin Luther King, Jr. "You don't have to see the whole staircase to take the first step." You start with one step. Then the next, and the next, until you're well into a story that will unfold over time.

> "Have a bias toward action—let's see something happen now. You can break that big plan into small steps and take the first step right away."
>
> —Indira Gandhi

The phrase "bias for action" from India's first and only female prime minister has become a mantra for many social entrepreneurs and activists. Author and entrepreneur Scott Belsky adds "relentless." It's a reminder that it's the daily grind toward the big idea that counts, the steady accomplishing. You see that in the life of anyone who's done anything important. Successful innovation is less about having good ideas than it is about showing up every day, plugging away, and making it happen. If we're passionate about a cause, what keeps us from success? Marketing guru Seth Godin says it's *resistance*. We have to overcome the resistance of our prehistoric brain stem, our "lizard brain," that is "responsible for revenge, fear, and anger." Because our lizard brain is afraid of failure and wants to remain unnoticed, it hates creativity.

> The resistance leads people to make suggestions that slow you down, suggestions that water down your idea, suggestions that lead to compromises that lead to design death.... It's that little voice in the back of your head, the "but" or the "what if" that speaks up at the crucial moment and defeats the joy and insight you brought to the project in the first place. It's the lizard that ruins your career, stunts your projects, and hinders your organization.[31]

Godin calls on us to fight the resistance by "shipping," putting your work out into the world and pushing the send button. Do it often, even if it's not perfect. Have a deadline and meet it. "If you and your organization are the ones (the only ones) that can get things done, close the sale, ship the product and make a difference, you're the linchpins—the ones we can't live without." If you watch documentaries about world-changers you only get hints of their real work and struggles, but when you're around them in the real world what you see mostly is the daily slog. It's that hero's daily bias towards action that leads to their achievements and makes their lives notable. What will ship this afternoon? What step can you check off by Friday? World change requires tenacity, often years or decades of it. "Show up, show up, show up, and after a while the muse shows up, too," says author Isabel Allende. "If she doesn't show up invited, eventually she just shows up."

Done is better than perfect

"Good judgment comes from experience, and experience—well, that comes from poor judgment."
—A.A. Milne

I'm on a plane in 1981. The guy in the next seat works for 3M. He shows me some little pads of paper, enthusiastically describing how useful they'll be in the work place. I remember being skeptical, thinking what would these be used for? Obviously, I was wrong: There may be a Post-it note within your reach right now. They were invented by accident when some 3M chemical engineers trying to make a super-strong adhesive managed to make a super-weak one instead. One of the engineers decided to try the adhesive paper as a bookmark in the hymnal as he sang in a church choir in St. Paul, Minnesota, and Post-it notes were born. Mistakes have given birth to plenty of inventions, including penicillin, pacemakers, and plastic. In 1853, Levi Strauss brought a bunch of canvas to San Francisco thinking he'd sell tents to gold prospectors. It turns out they preferred to sleep under the open sky, but what they really wanted was durable pants, so he turned his cloth into a new business. Ivory Soap was "invented" when a Procter and Gamble worker went to lunch and accidently left the mixer on. They shipped the defective bars anyway, and soon customers wanted more of the soap that floats. Rarely will our mistakes lead to some breakthrough product like these. And not all mistakes are equal, as Frank Lloyd Wright pointed out, "A doctor can bury his mistakes, but an architect can only advise his clients to plant vines." Some of our failures we just have to bury, others we fix what we can and keep moving. Fortunately, all are learning opportunities—at the very least telling us something doesn't work.

Maybe you've worked with someone who wouldn't let a project move forward until there was zero chance of anything going wrong. These kinds of folks can guarantee that little will happen: It's called paralysis by analysis. We avoid this and move with greater deliberation by accepting that we'll make mistakes along the way. If your idea can already improve some patch of the world, why put it in a box until it's fully developed? Why not toss it into the real world to see what happens… in the real world? It may be small at first but it's just getting started. Software developers use the term *Beta* when they release a new program or update before it's fully tested. Select customer/beta-testers feedback information that helps developers improve the program before the actual launch… *or* you could just go ahead and make the change and say it's *beta*. In *The Start-up of You*, LinkedIn cofounder Reid Hoffman and venture capitalist Ben Casnocha call this *permanent beta*. "Technology companies sometimes keep the beta test phase label on software for a time after the official launch to stress that the product is not finished so much as ready for the next batch of improvements," they say. "Gmail, for example, launched in 2004 but only left official beta in 2009, after millions of people were already using it. "[32] Put your ideas into the real world even before you have all the answers (which you'll never have). Do the best version you can with the time and resources you've got. You learn about the product as well as the processes needed to get it to market. The most valuable thing you'll get is the lessons. This worked great, but that sucked, so we'll change it.

"*Finished* ought to be an F-word for all of us," say Hoffman and Casnocha, "*We are all works in progress.* Each day presents an opportunity to learn more, do more, be more, grow more in our lives and careers." Benjamin Franklin said, "Well done is better than well said." Now we say action speaks louder than words. But *Done is better than perfect* is different; it's about finishing work and pushing it out the door. It's about not waiting until every conceivable flaw has been corrected. Not getting stuck. Finishing. The phrase became a mantra in Facebook's "hacker culture," described here in Mark Zuckerberg's letter to potential investors:

> Hackers try to build the best services over the long term by quickly releasing and learning from smaller iterations rather than trying to get everything right all at once. To support this, we have built a testing framework that at any given time can try out thousands of versions of Facebook. We have the words "Done is better than perfect" painted on our walls to remind ourselves to always keep shipping.

Is Paul McCartney's "Blackbird" done or perfect? I lean toward perfect. But most Beatles recordings (there are around 300) are simply done. Yet their combined effect was a fantastically creative body of work. In the early years, the group found its sound by performing in clubs relentlessly. When they were in song-writing mode, John Lennon and McCartney would schedule a series of days. Paul would drive to John's house and they'd get to work, "We always wrote a song a day, whatever happened we always wrote a song a day," he said. "We never had a dry day."[33] Had the Beatles performed only their perfect work perfectly, we'd have never heard of them. As you create projects and campaigns to improve the world, don't shoot for perfect: go for the done. Will any of your work be perfect? Probably not. Anne Lamott calls perfectionism "the voice of the oppressor, the enemy of the people."[34] Not surprisingly, if we're doing little because we're waiting for it to be perfect, our results will be nothing. People usually plug away for years before accomplishing anything big.

Here is the "Cult of the Done Manifesto,"[35] created by entrepreneur Bre Pettis and author Kio Stark, who gave themselves twenty minutes to write it:

The Cult of Done Manifesto

1. There are three states of being. Not knowing, action, and completion.

2. Accept that everything is a draft. It helps to get it done.

3. There is no editing stage.

4. Pretending you know what you're doing is almost the same as knowing what you are doing, so just accept that you know what you're doing even if you don't and do it.

5. Banish procrastination. If you wait more than a week to get an idea done, abandon it.

6. The point of being done is not to finish but to get other things done.

7. Once you're done you can throw it away.

8. Laugh at perfection. It's boring and keeps you from being done.

9. People without dirty hands are wrong. Doing something makes you right.

10. Failure counts as done. So, do mistakes.

11. Destruction is a variant of done.

12. If you have an idea and publish it on the internet, that counts as a ghost of done.

13. Done is the engine of more.

Starting over

"You're under no obligation to be the same person you were five minutes ago."

—Alan Watts

If you feel stuck, that things just aren't working, like an electronic gadget, it may be time to unplug and plug back in for a quick reboot. You take a vacation and you're off and running again. But it could be more. Maybe what you're doing isn't working. Maybe you're stuck. Maybe you want to better align with your values. Maybe you've got a great idea. Maintaining the current course may be dumber than making a fresh start. Peanuts cartoonist Charles Schulz once remarked, "Sometimes I lie awake at night, and I ask, 'Where have I gone wrong?' Then a voice says to me, 'This is going to take more than one night.'" Sleepless nights like these may tell us it's time for a new beginning. But if you've invested in something, even when it's floundering, it's hard to let go. Changing course can evoke a range of emotions, from fear to anticipation. And while it would be great if our *Plan A* always took us to success, it's been pointed out that if *Plan A* doesn't work, the alphabet has twenty-five more letters. An unsuccessful "A" can be a new opportunity. Starting over often means going to back to the drawing board.

In her junior year at Harvard, Jessica Matthews had a class assignment: Identify a need and then come up with a solution that included both art and science. Matthews and three other women formed a project team. Upon hearing their first idea about mobile health records, recalls Matthews, "Our professor said, *Meh!*" Fortunately, they weren't deep into their work, but they still had to come up with another concept, she told a group of students at the Clinton School of Public Service. "So, we locked ourselves in a room and started throwing out ideas." Although none of them had an engineering background, they thought of the quarter of the world's people who don't have reliable electricity. They decided to start with something people already enjoy, like soccer. Could a kicked ball capture kinetic energy and solve a power need? Armed with just high school physics, and told by engineers it wouldn't work, the students persisted. They built a prototype, a soccer ball that is a portable generator — thirty minutes of play could power a LED light for three hours. Their "sOccket ball" worked well enough to pass the course. Encouraged, they later developed a better version and tested it in South Africa. For the kids, having a soccer ball that created power was like magic. As a result of starting over, the team developed a winner. Matthews went on to co-found Uncharted Play, an organization that combines solving world problems and having fun.

The Statue of Liberty is a great symbol for the restart, inspiring the 12 million tired, poor, and yearning-to-be-free people who came through the immigration center on nearby Ellis Island. For different reasons, immigrants then and today are people dissatisfied with their current situation—whatever and wherever that is. Often, their very lives are at stake. They weigh the costs, take the risks, and leave behind the old, familiar life to reach a place of new, greater promise. That's our story too as world-changers. When it's time to reboot, we learn from and honor the good that came from the first effort, and find a way to say goodbye to the past to signal the shift. In restarting, you are now building a different future.

A room with a long view

Everyone loves a room with a view, one that overlooks a beautiful harbor, a quaint village, or a mountain range. But one room has arguably the best view in the world, and you can visit it for free. It's the assembly room at Independence Hall in Philadelphia, with its wood floors, high ceiling, and simple chairs and tables. The spectacular view isn't looking out the large, perfectly proportioned windows. The great view is the one that looks forward. In this room during the troubled summer of 1776, a small group of citizens passionately debated their future. Today we call them "founding fathers," but at the time they were activists and revolutionaries who created and signed—at risk of death—a declaration of independence from a powerful tyrant king across the ocean. In signing their names, they launched the American experiment in democracy. After a long war, the colonists prevailed, and during the summer of 1787, a second group gathered in that same room to hammer out a structure that would bind the thirteen independent states into one nation. From the start, this experiment was flawed: Written by White men of privilege, the Constitution structured a government that protected slavery. To keep the less populated states on board, it gave them disproportionate power, creating electoral challenges that distort our democracy to this day. People who didn't own property couldn't vote. Women couldn't vote. For electoral purposes, each slave counted as three-fifths of a person. Of course, they couldn't vote and were considered property. Plenty was egregiously wrong. It was a simply a bunch of folks under extreme pressure doing the best they could that hot summer.

Imperfect as it was, somehow, they got a great deal of it right. What gives this room its spectacular view is its *long* look. Over the decades, people of this nation have been in a nonstop struggle, sometimes bloody, to bring to each person the ideals on the two documents signed in this room. "We the people," "promote the general welfare," "all men are created equal," "unalienable rights," "life, liberty, and the pursuit of happiness." Certainly, those in Independence Hall would be shocked to see the long tail of their deliberations. Over time, the American experiment they birthed inspired movements among people across the planet. It still does. Recent anti-democratic movements tell us the crucial work begun in that room is far from done. Of course, equally inspiring people have bravely struggled for freedom, rights, and justice in every corner of the world. And there are thousands of other rooms to see. Start with the small prison cell on Robbins Island where Nelson Mandela spent eighteen years for his fight against South African apartheid. Fortunately, this very day similar rooms are near each one of us—rooms where citizens are struggling to overcome some injustice, trying to create a better society. And these rooms are calling us. While we aren't obligated to get it perfect, we are obligated to *do something*, to join in, to act, and set up a better place for the generations coming behind us.

CHAPTER FIVE

Grow your cause

Grow your cause by doing two seemingly opposite things at once. First, incrementally improve the programs, revenue streams, branding, public relations, and so on, that already work well or at least have potential. At the same time, constantly look for those breakthrough ideas that can take you to a new place.

Constant improvement: *kaizen* and flywheels

Incremental change is often criticized for being too slow and simply doing more of the same. In fact, it can be wildly powerful. The Japanese developed *kaizen*—it means *good change*—the idea of continuous improvement. Using kaizen in manufacturing, engineering, quality improvement, assembly, and other practices, they incrementally made better and better products. The practice of kaizen took their economy to new heights and dislodged U.S. automakers and other manufacturers from their long-time dominance. Now it's more of a philosophy of constantly making small improvements to any kind of work, changes that over time add up to create dramatic results. In *Good to Great* Jim Collins uses the flywheel to describe a related key practice found in successful companies. Collins asks us to picture a giant "massive metal disk mounted horizontally on an axle, about 30 feet in diameter, two feet thick, and weighing 5,000 pounds. Now your task is to get the flywheel rotating on the axle as fast and long as possible."[36] It takes a lot of energy, pushing hard, to get it moving a little bit. And after great effort the flywheel makes one rotation. You push again and again to keep it turning. After a while it's a bit easier, until finally the flywheel seems to spin on its own at a high speed. That's how doing anything worth doing happens: It can be slow and hard, but eventually, if you keep pushing and improve steadily, you achieve momentum.

Like many nonprofits, Heifer International used direct mail to raise funds. And since the 1970s, among the mailings it sent was an early version of the "gift catalog." You could call this mail program a breakthrough. It was different from the mail other groups sent because it offered symbolic gifts that were given to friends and family during the holidays. For example, you could give a goat or a cow in someone's name. The real animal wouldn't show up under the Christmas tree (to everyone's relief!), but would arrive in a village where a struggling family had been trained in small-scale livestock management. When I arrived at Heifer in 1992, the gift catalog mailing program wasn't attracting that much in donations. For a decade, Heifer's total revenue had been flat at about $5 million a year. When adjusted for inflation that meant Heifer had lost half of its spending power. In the seventies and eighties, the catalog direct mail program had no traction. The real growth began in the early nineties as we began a string of improvements that, over time, got the flywheel spinning. Each year, we made a new push or two: adding color, better stories and photos, more efficient production and distribution, better publicity. We rented and mailed to other groups' lists to get new supporters. Mike Matchett, who headed our marketing, wondered about the rate we paid to process each credit card donation. Negotiating a slightly lower rate freed up hundreds of thousands of dollars for the mission. (Understanding the potential for savings in the often overlooked back-office, Mike later founded NonprofitRate.com, a curated catalog of discounts and resources for nonprofits and change-makers.) One early flywheel push came to me as an *aha* while sitting in my yard. Growing up in Texas, I was aware of the Neiman Marcus holiday catalog that was mailed every year. It always included one outrageously priced item like his and her camels or a mini-submarine. So why not add to our catalog an outrageously priced donation: a $5,000 Gift Ark? As for Neiman Marcus, it was good for publicity. More important, it was good for the bottom line: It didn't take too many Gift Arks to raise the average gift. People, schools, and congregations got excited about the challenge and the good they knew they could support. We added celebrity quotes and photos of people like Susan Sarandon and Walter Cronkite posing with llamas and sheep. We found an innovative data process that helped us mail to people who were more likely to donate. All told, we added around two dozen unique and significant improvements, and each one (once tested and proven) became another push on the flywheel, causing it to spin faster and faster. Even before we were aware of the flywheel metaphor, we practiced it. The approach played a big role in how my team at Heifer International grew our annual marketing revenue from $3 million to $90 million. "The flywheel image captures the overall feel of what it was like inside the companies as they went from good to great," says Collins.

> No matter how dramatic the end result, the good-to-great transformations never happened in one fell swoop. There was no single defining action, no grand program, no one killer innovation, no solitary lucky break, no wrenching revolution. Good to great comes about by a cumulative process—step by step, action by action, decision, turn by turn of the flywheel—that adds up to sustained and spectacular results.[37]

This approach can help you grow your cause. Chances that you'll soon find a new breakthrough way to raise giant sums for your cause are not high. But your chances through constant improvement *over time* to develop ways to raise giant sums are actually good. Keep at it and practice kaizen. Look for and test a way to improve your core activities. By the time that improvement is made you should already be started on the next one, leading you on a trajectory of powerful growth.

Breakthroughs, game-changers

Under Steve Jobs, Apple created an unparalleled chain of breakthroughs. Every few years, they would disrupt an entire market by launching a game-changing product: the computer industry with the Mac's intuitive, easy-to-use graphic interface that ordinary people would want in their home; the music industry with the iPod, a small device that stored thousands of songs; and the cell phone industry with the iPhone. While they are rare, breakthroughs can change things. Heifer International's gift catalog was also a breakthrough. It's a mash-up of a year-end fundraising appeal and colorful holiday gift catalog. Shown photos of dairy cows, chickens, and other livestock, along with their farmer families, donors were asked to make a symbolic holiday gift to help others get food- and income-producing animals.

After a few years, the success of this fundraising approach started showing up on the radar of other nonprofits. In the ironically competitive world of fundraising, many groups jumped on the bandwagon. Suddenly, everyone was in the livestock business. One international nonprofit quickly mailed a gift catalog with goats on the cover, even though they had no livestock projects. A denominational agency that was represented on our board got caught lifting sentences about chickens directly from our catalog into theirs. This wasn't just happening at home. Seeing the success of our U.K. partner, Send a Cow, in just one year about two dozen nonprofits in the United Kingdom mailed out their first gift catalogs. Some succeeded and many failed. Today, nonprofits around the world raise funds through gift catalogs. Just as important, the attractive format helps them get the word out about their important missions. A group that is first to market with a new product or service often benefits from "first mover advantage," which helps with brand recognition and customer loyalty. Not only did Heifer have the first mover advantage in this new approach, but it had a fifty-year-old, proven, sustainable livestock program that happened to lend itself to the format: great photos of wonderful farmers around the world (I've met quite a few myself) happily posing with their goats and water buffalo.

Some challenges demand a breakthrough. "We don't have the time to incrementally increase," said Homegrown National Park's Michelle Alfandari, referring to the climate crisis. "There's no slow build here. We can't double, we have to grow exponentially." About one thousand people a month are currently adding their patches of land to HNP's online map showing they are planting native species and reducing the invasive plants. "A thousand a month sounds good, but at that rate, it'll take us about 4,030 years to reach our goal," added Doug Tallamy. "We have to do things in fast motion."

Innovation never travels a predictable road. But while there are no guarantees, you can increase your odds of finding a breakthrough with processes such as asset mapping or appreciative inquiry. We'll look at some of these in chapter 8. Sometimes breakthroughs just appear. You may get a sudden *aha!* idea in the shower or in a dream. But most of them come to those who obsess, whatever that looks like, and only long after they've paid homage to the gods of frustration and real-world struggle.

The yin and yang of incremental change and breakthrough live in tension. In *Focus: The Hidden Driver of Excellence*, psychologist Daniel Goleman describes this in terms of *exploitation* and *exploration*:

Exploration means we disengage from a current focus to search for new possibilities, and allows flexibility, discovery, and innovation. Exploitation takes sustained focus on what you're already doing, so you can refine efficiencies and improve performance. Those who exploit can find a safer path to profits, while those who explore can potentially find a far greater success in the next new thing—though the risks of failure are greater, and the horizon of payback is further away. Exploitation is the tortoise, exploration the hare.[38]

Balance the needs. While Apple's breakthroughs built their success, so did the kaizen. Each year devotees swarm the Apple events to see what improvements have been made on existing products, to watch the next turn of the flywheel. Blend these two and flourish!

Marketing for growth

Not too long ago, many nonprofits looked askance at the idea of *marketing*. In the mid-nineties, when Heifer International's revenue had not grown for ten years, I worked with Michael Cervino, who had helped grow Habitat for Humanity, to create a marketing plan, based on the results of some direct mail tests. It mapped how we could grow the annual marketing revenue from about $3 million a year to $20 million in five years. Excited to share this good news with the board of directors, I walked them through the plan step by step, starting with the results of our testing and the early growth. I then waited for their enthusiastic response. Nope, that wasn't going to happen. As someone in the room said later, had you seen their reaction you'd have thought I'd just pissed on the table! First, they didn't like the word *marketing*. It was not politically correct. Marketing was what immoral corporations did to manipulate unsuspecting people into buying things they didn't need. Second, they'd gotten behind previous leaders who had given this kind of revenue growth pep talk, but it didn't work. Finally, at that time there was almost no business experience, much less marketing, on the board. They couldn't recognize that this plan was based on data from testing. I obviously did a poor job of messaging that day; I certainly didn't know my audience well enough. It never occurred to me that the board would have any reason to object to growth. After all, the program in the field worked great, helping people overcome hunger and poverty. But we never had enough money. Eventually, we kept at the marketing and they came around. We wildly surpassed the numbers set out in that plan and kept growing for many years, becoming one of the fastest growing nonprofits. Fifteen years later, not only had we grown that marketing revenue to $90 million a year but we had also created a brand that had buzz and was loved and supported by millions of donors.

Nonprofits often begin with the support of the friends and family of those with the original idea, but at some point, it becomes clear that the opportunity is greater than this original group can handle. Many turn to marketing to raise more funds, recruit more supporters and volunteers, and extend the program. Most use the approaches that businesses have developed over time, including direct mail, online marketing, branding, special campaigns, and public relations. Perhaps the most widely-used framework for this is the "Four P's of Marketing." This workhorse since the 1940s is used to design marketing programs with a "marketing mix" that's blended to get the desired objectives from the target market. The goal is to put the right product in the right place at the right price at the right time! The *Product* can be tangible: a car or spinach. Or it could be a service: a tourist experience, data search, dry cleaning. The brand comes in here, along with the appearance and packaging. How is your product presented? How is it different? What need does it satisfy? How is it designed, how easy is it to use? *Place* involves where someone gets the product or service. In stores, online, on street corners? What are the issues around distribution, inventory, warehousing, processing, transportation, and so on?

Price involves what the customer or client pays. List price, discounts, pricing strategy, market share, profit per unit? What does your product or service cost your organization to deliver? *Promotion*. What is the messaging to the buyers or donors? To clients? How do you use advertising, media, PR, and personal selling? How are target audiences told about the product: TV, radio, social media, print, in person? Of course, the temptation was too great, so folks quickly added to the original four P's such tools as *people*: customer experience and other human aspects; *process*: how customers and business interact; *physical evidence*: buildings as the places of interaction, ambiance, packaging, and all artifacts; *policy*: rules and regulations that impact your products or services. Mix and test these P's to find ways to grow your cause. This framework sets the stage for further questions: How are you going to get your message and call to action to your target audience? Which channels will be most effective? To reach your audience should you start with an email or a billboard?

Social marketing to save the crabs

While most marketing tries to persuade us to buy something, social marketing has a different purpose. U.S. advertisers spend well over $200 billion a year to expose us to countless ads in their quest to, as clinical psychologist and author Mary Pipher puts it, "convince us to buy stuff we mostly don't need or want."[39] She elaborates in *Writing to Save the World*, "Cigarettes and alcohol are depicted as refreshing. Ads miseducate our children about the nature of happiness, teaching them just the opposite of what all the world's great religions teach… that to feel good you need to buy something you do not need." She quotes George Carlin: "Trying to be happy by accumulating possessions is like trying to satisfy hunger by taping sandwiches all over your body." Noting the thousands of ads we see every day, she asks us rather to imagine those messages encouraging us to eat more fruits and vegetables, brush our teeth, call our great aunt, and behave kindly toward one another. What she's talking about is *social marketing*.

Besides raising support to carry out the mission, many non-profits engage in social marketing: trying to persuade people to change their behavior in ways that help society (and themselves). Well-known for encouraging us to prevent wildfires on billboards across the U.S., Smokey the Bear could *also* serve as the poster child for social marketing. Millions have changed habits because of campaigns that urged us to buckle up for safety, say no to drugs, recycle, use condoms, don't let friends drive drunk, eat more fruits and vegetables, keep America beautiful. Those campaigns that succeed create significant measurable progress in society. In their book *Social Marketing*[40] Philip Kotler and Nancy Lee list some distinguishing characteristics of this strategy: "Focus on behaviors. Behavior change is typically voluntary. Use of traditional marketing principals and techniques. Select and influence a target market. Primary beneficiary is society."

A recent news article should give us reason to cheer: A study found that the Chesapeake Bay dead zones are coming back to life. Dead zones happen when nutrient pollution, especially chemical fertilizers, run downstream into large bodies of water and deplete the oxygen, killing off much of the marine life. But programs to reduce fertilizer, animal waste, and other pollutants are now bringing life back to the Chesapeake Bay. Kotler and Lee describe one such creative campaign to convince residents around the bay to change when they fertilize their yards. Lawn fertilizer runoff was devastating the bay's ecosystem as residents fertilized in the spring when the heavy rains washed much of the chemicals into the bay. How could the social marketers get people to switch to the fall? "Lawn care partners were a critical part of the strategy. Messages to fertilize in the fall would fail if there was no fertilizer available in the fall," Kotler and Lee reported. So these companies were convinced to join up. Brochures, clever ads for both print and television, and a website were developed explaining the campaign and branding it as The Chesapeake Club to "create a sense of membership, participation, and practice of a behavior that is the accepted social norm…. Mass media messaging focused on 'wait until fall to fertilize,'" say the authors. The Chesapeake Club reframed the issue as culinary, focusing on the iconic Blue Crab. They engaged with local lawn care companies, restaurants. and others to encourage the club's clever "Save the Crabs. Then Eat 'Em" campaign. That slogan was printed on drink coasters, as Kotler and Lee describe:

> …and distributed without charge to local seafood restaurants to use and hand out to patrons. The coasters sported the "fertilize in the fall" message on the back, and waitstaff were informed regarding the purpose of the campaign and why fall fertilizing is more environmentally sound. In this way, restaurants also became partners in disseminating the campaign message and, as an extra incentive, were also promoted on the campaign website.[41]

All of this took place alongside supporting media. The results were measured: The campaign successfully raised awareness and helped many residents switch from spring to fall fertilizing, thus reducing pollution in the bay.

Getting to the right folks

For a dozen years, I've taught marketing for nonprofits at the Clinton School of Public Service. As part of their work, each student creates a marketing plan for a real organization. A few weeks in, I check to see how the plans are coming along. Almost every year, despite what they should have read in our textbooks and what I had already said in class several times, this conversation takes place:

Me: Who are you trying to reach with this effort? Who is your audience?

Student: Everyone!

Too many fundraisers say the same thing. Naturally, we want everyone who hears of our good work to support our cause, but marketers know there's no *everybody*, no general public. Try to speak to everyone and you speak to no one. Even if you won some magic lottery that gave you unlimited resources to reach everybody you're still better off focusing. Depending on your cause, you may need help from a variety of people: members, donors, volunteers, journalists to spread the word, people to attend events, advocates to sign petitions. You may want people to adopt animals, donate old furniture, or attend the symphony. Financial supporters differ: Some will write a large check, some will give $10 online, and some only want to go to the big gala. They all represent different audiences. So, who is your *target* audience? How do you narrow it down from "everybody"? First, what does your cause absolutely need from many others to accomplish its mission? Is it funds, publicity, labor, something else? From your many answers, narrow it down to one singular need, which should drive your chief marketing goal. The folks who can help you meet this need are your target audience. Start by knowing these folks in real life. But also understand their age, gender, education level, where they live (demographics); their interests, lifestyles, and attitudes (psychographics). Delve deeply into what they care about, what they aspire to. The better you know someone the more effective you'll be. If you've done your work well, your cause will be good news to these folks. Focus the lion's share of your communications here. "The aim of marketing is to know and understand the customer so well the product or service fits him [or her] and sells itself," says Peter Drucker. To grow your cause, figure out how to connect with the right people.

You may occasionally receive in the mail a packet of coupons from a store where you shop that includes items you've already bought there: 25 percent off spices, 15 percent off pillows, 20 percent off sliced jalapeños. These coupons aren't random. Stores track what we buy and custom print a unique set of coupons—with a picture of each item—in a brochure for an only-person-in-the-universe audience: you. Now, you may not have the technology to pinpoint your supporters' needs with this level of precision—although the honing tools are increasingly available and affordable—but you *can* adjust your messaging based on what you *do* know about them.

You probably have a few other mission-critical communication bases you need to cover, perhaps with foundations or local media. These secondary markets don't deserve the same level of attention. Certainly, you need to communicate with them, addressing their special needs, but save the big efforts for your target audience. Your core message doesn't change, but how you speak with different groups may vary widely. Early in my time at Heifer International, we asked donors in surveys and focus groups why they supported our organization. With no prompting they overwhelmingly responded that they wanted to help families become self-reliant. While not surprising, it was essential that we understood this. From that point, we made sure that self-reliance was central to every message. But when we spoke with congregations, we added faith language and spoke of moral imperatives. To foundations we talked about impact and included evaluation data. Our holiday gift catalog questioned whether Uncle Al needed another tie and included the cool factor of alternative gifts for family and friends. But all of our communications spoke of how the livestock and training transformed lives and helped families move toward self-reliance.

Much is written about marketing to different age segments, such as the greatest generation, boomers, and Gen Z. These and other types of groupings should inform your language choices. An appeal that works with retirees may bomb with teenage boys. Even though you are describing the same cause and making the same call to action, it may sound different. Major gift fundraisers take the time to understand that single potential donor's interests, and their communication with that donor reflects those specific interests, with the message adjusted to a target audience of one. Music performers joke about the difference between a rock musician and a jazz musician. A rocker plays three chords in front of three thousand people while a jazz musician plays three thousand chords in front of three. Depending on the audience, your message may sound different even though you're playing the same tune. The song is your core message: How it's performed or communicated can change. Craft messages to the concerns of your target audience.

The marketing exchange: cookies for...

One day driving on a busy street in my neighborhood, I noticed a couple of kids in their yard holding up signs, flagging down cars. A few adults sat nearby in lawn chairs watching and laughing. I was about to keep going when I realized what was happening: They were selling Girl Scout cookies! Immediately, the combination of cute kids being entrepreneurs and the anticipated taste of a Thin Mint kicked in. I parked and bought a few boxes. Kids marketing cookies. In 2014, thirteen-year-old Danielle Lee took this to a new level when she planted her cookie sales in front of a medical marijuana shop in San Francisco and sold 117 boxes in two hours. Anticipating copycats, the Colorado Girl Scout officials quickly nipped this marketing idea in the bud and warned their girls: none of that! They pointed out that the kids couldn't set up outside strip bars, liquor stores, or any other adult-oriented businesses. Fair enough. But these stories raise questions for those who market for causes: How do you legitimately tap into real needs, perceived needs, or wants? Does anyone truly need three boxes of Thin Mint cookies? The primitive-lizard part of our brain tells us, *Yes, we do!* But another voice tells us those cookies don't fit into our plan to eat healthy. Okay, so the cookies fall more into the *want* category. Of course, everyone *wants* to support the worthy Girl Scouts. Whatever motives are tapped, the cookies sell—200 million boxes worth about $800 million a year.[42]

The *marketing exchange* is about trading: I give something that benefits you and you give something that benefits me. When goods (tangible), services (intangible), ideas or money are traded, each party gets something of value from the other. The marketing exchange for even a cup of coffee isn't always simple. You want a cup of coffee and a shop has coffee for sale. You buy a cup. But hold on, if you live or work nearby, you could have made a whole pot at a fraction of the cost. So what's up? Maybe you can't make a cappuccino at home, or maybe you really just wanted to get out, to meet friends, or to do your work around other people. So, you are partly buying that third place beyond home and the office. And maybe you'll pay more if it's fair trade coffee, because you care about the livelihood of the farmers who grew it. The creativity of benefit marketing exchange went into overdrive at the height of the COVID-19 pandemic as state and local governments and others laid out goodies to encourage the vaccine-hesitant. The Talladega Superspeedway in Alabama offered two laps around the track for anyone willing to get the shot. Around the country, folks were given tickets to places like Six Flags and events like Yankees games. For many it was a cash bonus of $100. In Arkansas, it was hunting and fishing licenses. Many states offered lottery incentives, including California's ten chances to win $1.5 million. And to come full circle, Indiana gave out boxes of Girl Scout cookies!

Aspirin marketing, aspiration marketing

Nonprofit or cause marketers are looking for a donation, volunteer support, a "share" on social media, a behavior change (getting vaccinated or not smoking), or action for advocacy. In these exchanges, unlike commercial businesses, supporters typically don't get anything tangible back. Often, it's just a good feeling! This makes world-change marketing more challenging. Good feelings may suffice for some, but if you want to build a sustainable, growing base, consider giving something back that your supporter wants—or even better—needs!

In a *Fast Company* column, "Turning Vitamins into Aspirins,"[43] educators, authors, and brothers Dan and Chip Heath suggest that you're better off selling aspirins than vitamins. "Vitamins are nice; they're healthy. But aspirin cures your pain; it's not a nice-to-have, it's a must-have." We're tempted to believe that support for our programs will come pouring in because a newly-created fundraising campaign shows our cause to be worthy. But from the potential supporter's perspective it may be a mere vitamin, not something they need now. When you send a fundraising letter, you're appealing to your audience's various needs. Again, think marketing exchange: maybe you're tapping into their sense of duty or a simple desire to help solve a social challenge. But the Heath brothers start with the question, *What do you really need, right now?* You may have a slamming headache; how can we eliminate your pain? If you can find a way to meet a big need of your supporters as they help you, you'll do twice as well and take your organization to a new level.

For example, what might a congregational youth leader need? Several fun and meaningful programs each year that reinforce faith values, make kids glad they showed up, and make the youth leader look good. If your organization can create a fundraising program that also provides that aspirin, the youth group will raise $5,000 for you and feel great about it. I know, we've created several programs that did just that. Everyone wins, including the youth who had fun, hopefully learned something, and saw they could actually make a difference. Another possibility: It's early December and the holiday shopper feels the need to buy gifts for ten people, and soon. A nonprofit's catalog arrives in the mail asking them to donate to help drill a water well for a village or buy a dairy goat for milk for a struggling family in honor of someone on their holiday gift list. They realize that five of the people on their list don't need more stuff but would love to be honored in this way. Those five will get a nice card explaining the gift and the shopper can avoid the mall. This catalog moved from a mere fundraising appeal to actually helping solve an immediate need. Or a schoolteacher may be interested in a program that gets kids to read lots of books at that critical point when reading can become a habit. Through sponsors for each book students read, the program also raises funds for a nonprofit. Just as important, the children experience helping others. We did all of these at Heifer, actually meeting many people's real needs while they helped others.

Homegrown National Park offers an entire packet of aspirins. For the person wanting to make a real-world improvement on the environment, here you go. For the gardener who has already gone down the native plant path a bit, here's a tribe of others like you: community, along with some resources to help you and stories to encourage you. For the person trying to buy native plants in their area, here's a growing directory of those who sell them—or give them away for free. For the company or organization wanting to do something meaningful with their campus grounds, here's a plan (and a way to get on the doing-good map). Perhaps most important, for the one who'd rather do anything else than mow the lawn on a hot Saturday in July, come on in. There's room for you. And you're about to be enjoying nature a lot more.

Create an *ecosystem of winners*. When a friend of mine needed some blinds for his window, we stopped into the local Habitat for

Humanity ReStore. There he found a brand-new set of wooden blinds for only $15, a real bargain! The giant warehouse-sized store in North Carolina was full of new and gently-used home items: furniture, doors, windows, washers and driers, lighting, plumbing, and more. From its small beginnings in 1976 in Americus, Georgia, Habitat for Humanity has grown to become one of the top ten homebuilders in the United States (and most Habitat houses are built in other countries). While a brick-and-mortar outlet doesn't make sense for every cause, ReStore outlets make great sense for Habitat. It's right in its space: home construction. The more than eight hundred stores around the country are owned and operated by the local Habitat affiliates. The ReStore ecosystem has many winners. Customers, also known as bargain hunters, can buy things they need for their home at a fraction of the cost. Furnishings and home repair become easier for people on limited incomes. Individuals can donate things they want to move out of the house after spring cleaning or remodeling. Most stores will pick up the larger items. Builders can donate their excess materials and supplies...or pick up bargains. Companies can also do good by donating excess stock or other items (and get a tax break). For example, in a two-year period, Whirlpool donated $10 million in appliances to ReStores. Volunteers are rewarded by working "from customer service to furniture repair," says the Habitat website. Low-income families win as they move into a house built by themselves and volunteers, and funded in part with the revenue of ReStore sales. Of course, that's the reason Habitat exists. The local environments are improved as recycling diverts tons of materials from landfills each year. Even struggling neighborhoods can benefit, as some ReStores are new businesses in economically- challenged areas. Of course, the Habitat for Humanity house-building program is another winner ecosystem. Volunteers get to literally roll up their sleeves and build something, a do-gooder's dream. At the end of the day, they can see what they've done. They can also learn building skills to use on their own homes. Deserving low-income families add a great deal of sweat-equity, putting many hours into building their houses. They also pay a mortgage. And they end up with a new, affordable home. Communities are helped as targeted neighborhoods see new life. Companies can donate goods and engage their employees, and the list of winners goes on. What needs could be met while people support your cause? What "must-have" can your group give your potential supporter?

And then there's *aspiration* marketing. Interviewing then President Barack Obama from his Los Angeles podcasting garage, Marc Maron asked about the 2008 campaign posters on *Hope* and *Change*. Obama said "Those are capturing aspirations about where we should be going—a society that's more just, a society that's more equal, a society in which the dignity of every individual is respected, a society of tolerance, a society of opportunity," said Obama. "The question then is how do you operationalize those abstract concepts into something really concrete? How do we get somebody a job? How do we improve a school? How do we make sure that everybody gets decent healthcare? As soon as you start talking about specifics then—the world's complicated—there are choices you have to make." Obama's 2008 campaign resonated not with sharing nitty-gritty plans but by speaking to the aspirations of voters who wanted to see a better day. While it quickly gets "complicated," significant change begins with aspiration, a strong desire or hope to achieve something important. You may aspire to be the mayor, to own a home, earn a degree, open a bakery. You may aspire to be a better parent, give more generously, work harder, or be more relaxed. We all have aspirations and so do your potential supporters. Listen to them and learn whether their aspirations align with your cause, and how. Then you can go deeper than that hunger for Girl Scout cookies. Help your supporters achieve something they hope for.

A good revenue mix

If your cause gets most of its funds from just one source, you should meet some farmers I visited in a small South African town. Anna and William Matidza practice integrated farming. On their half acre they grow tomatoes, cabbage, sugar cane, and onions for the family to eat and to sell in the village market. They sell papaya, peach, mulberries, mango, citrus, and guava from trees they planted. With their profits they have added some irrigation and a piggery. Yes, the pigs provide meat, but they give another benefit: The Matidzas used to buy one hundred fifty bags of manure a year to fertilize their garden but now they have plenty at no cost. By local standards, they do well with their diverse food and revenue. Why some of their neighbors (who can see their success) don't do the same puzzles the Matidzas.

In monocropping, you grow one crop (like corn) that usually requires costly fertilizers and pesticides that harm the environment. If a disease, drought, or unexpected price drop hits that crop, you're out of luck. A healthy farm, however, is a mix of enterprises that support each other: manure enriches the soil for grasses and crops, which in turn feed the animals. Bees provide honey and pollination, often doubling crop yields. There's a proper place for nature, for songbirds, and other wildlife. When one enterprise has a bad year, others make up for it. Like a sustainable farm, your nonprofit's mix of enterprises can create growth and sustainability. Most of your revenue probably comes from one or two programs. By all means, keep building these programs; they're your bread and butter. But be sure to diversify as well.

Another reason is to help you discover your cash cow. Many nonprofits are struggling because they haven't yet found their big, signature fundraising program—an online campaign, an annual event, a niche for government grants. Authors William Foster and Gail Fine talked with leaders of some of the largest nonprofits and reported their findings in *Stanford Social Innovation Review*.[44] "Only a few of the twenty-one interviewees knew from the start where they would find their most promising funding sources," they report. "But as these organizations pursued their growth, they realized which sources of funding seemed most promising and were willing to concentrate their efforts on that source, recruiting people and creating organizations that could best pursue that funding source." Over time, incubating several fundraising programs—with regular tweaking—will help you discover that big revenue stream, the one that will drive growth. Keep the others that are working, but give special focus to the cash cow.

Diverse revenue streams can also feed each other through cross-marketing, so that one plus one equals three. Some of the people who join in that large pool of supporters created by mass marketing will become major donors or help you create a corporate partnership. They may introduce your cause to their congregation, school, or a foundation. But you must first develop donor programs that match the needs of these groups. That school program can generate many small first-time gifts from potentially long-term donors. A grant or corporate gift can add to your credibility. As potential supporters see you in more places, the relationship is deepened, the brand reinforced.

Mentioned earlier, diverse revenue can lessen the chances of a financial disaster. Nonprofits and businesses of all sorts and sizes struggled with the unexpected COVID-19 shutdowns and restrictions. For many, quickly adding new sources of funds was a matter of survival. Distraction by a catastrophe—like September 11 or a natural disaster—just as you're mailing that one big appeal or hosting your signature event could wipe out your chances of reaching revenue goals. So, practice integrated fundraising to discover your most promising revenue source and to learn how your various fundraising programs can strengthen each other.

CHAPTER SIX

The mighty message

"Give me twenty-six lead soldiers and I will conquer the world."

What is the most powerful human force? Some say it's reason, some say love, some say cooperation. They have one thing in common, they all depend on communication. As a force for good, so does your cause. This starts with a relationship—knowing and understanding your audience—and is followed by figuring out the best way to get the best message to them. Equally important? To hear them as well. "Give me twenty-six lead soldiers and I will conquer the world." Referring to printing press lead type of bygone days, this quote about the power of the printed word has been attributed to both Benjamin Franklin and Karl Marx. And both of them marshalled those lead soldiers to make serious dents in history. Franklin co-authored the Declaration of Independence, helping set loose the practice of democracy. But he also popularized what has become a $10 billion industry: self-improvement. At age twenty, he published his *13 Virtues for a Better Life*, beginning with Temperance: "Eat not to dullness; drink not to elevation." And while he didn't always live by his own advice, he never stopped publishing it. In 1848, Karl Marx, along with Fredrich Engels, published *The Communist Manifesto*. And over the next century-and-a-half, their ideas (however mangled) did, in fact, conquer about half of the world. The alphabet army formed into compelling ideas is formidable. From marine biologist Rachel Carson, who launched an environmental movement with her book *Silent Spring*, to thousands of citizens leaning into social media to launch Arab Spring, people of every kind are changing our world through words.

Audience is hero

Nancy Duarte has worked on thousands of presentations, most notably Al Gore's "An Inconvenient Truth." In *Resonate*, a book I recommend more than any other, she draws on Gore's talk and the speeches of people like Ronald Reagan, Martha Graham, and Abraham Lincoln to show what makes a presentation powerful and compelling. If you're trying to change the world, perhaps the most important advice comes from Duarte: "You are not the hero who will save the audience, the audience is your hero." *Audience is hero* has become a mantra among people I work with and in my classes. This shift in how we understand our role can transform our ability to connect with potential supporters and allies. So, if you or your organization is not the hero, then what is your role? "You are the mentor. You're Yoda, not Luke Skywalker," explains Duarte. "The audience is the one who'll do all the heavy lifting to help you reach your objectives. You're simply the one voice helping them get unstuck in their journey."[45] Mentors, she says, offer the hero "guidance, confidence, insight, advice, training, or magical gifts so he can overcome his initial fears and enter into the new journey with you." From this more humble perspective, the compelling presentation is not about the presenter, nor their organization. Rather, it's about why and how audience members can take up the cause. Challenge your audience to embark on an adventure—a hero's journey—and then provide some help for that journey. This goes well beyond presentations; the audience should be the hero in your brochures, email appeals, and videos. Whether you're asking someone to make a donation, volunteer, or support a piece of legislation, the people you're talking with will choose whether to take action. The one who joins is now the protagonist. The cause has moved farther along.

Of course, you will find often yourself speaking with those who are already on board: preaching to the choir. They are the loyal superfans who keep showing up, the heartbeat of your cause. For them, the message may be more sophisticated and nuanced, but you are still telling them how much they are valued. In *Writing to Change the World*, Mary Pipher tells us that, in fact, "most preaching *is* to the choir":

> Choirs produce almost all the important social action in our world. The people most likely to read us are the people who think like we do. And readers generally seek reinforcement of their beliefs, not arguments or challenges. When writing for compatriots, we hope to energize and sustain them. We want to deliver new thoughts and information to them, strengthen their beliefs and mobilize them to action. Often, we will cite common history and heroes, and employ shared, meaning-laden metaphors. This kind of "to the barricades" writing enjoins communities of believers to make things happen.[46]

Your cause's unfinished work is for those in the audience. Duarte also says that effective speeches move back and forth from a bad current situation, or *what is*, to a vision of a better future, *what could be*. The speaker invites the listener: Help us bring about a better future by taking a specific action. Help us make this vision of *what could be* a reality! She points to one of America's most famous speeches. In his address commemorating the battle at Gettysburg, President Lincoln said that the brave soldiers had already dedicated the land they were there to consecrate. So he turned his remarks to the audience of those still alive:

> It is for us, the living, rather to be dedicated here to the unfinished work which they have, thus far, so nobly carried on. It is rather for us to be here dedicated to the great task remaining before us—that from these honored dead we take increased devotion to that cause for which they gave the last full measure of devotion—that we here highly resolve that these dead shall not have died in vain; that this nation shall have a new birth of freedom; and that this government of the people, by the people, for the people, shall not perish from the earth.

Yes, heroes died on the battlefield to save the "new nation, conceived in liberty," but those gathered are needed to be the next heroes, to rededicate themselves to the unfinished work of freedom. Like Lincoln, describe the next step for your audience and invite them to take it.

Get your message through

How many times do we need to put our message out there to be effective? Marketing consultant and author Roy Williams[47] recounts being told by a friend, "I'm sending you the best book ever written on selling." Williams couldn't wait, and when the FedEx package arrived, he told his assistant he was taking the afternoon to read. He then tells of his anger and disbelief when he found a copy of Dr. Seuss' Green Eggs and Ham. At first, he thought his friend was a practical joker. But when he sat and read the book, he realized his friend was, in fact, a genius. Sam-I-Am is a great salesperson as he tries to persuade his "customer" to eat green eggs and ham: Would he eat them in a box or with a fox? The average sale comes after only five asks, says Williams, while Sam-I-Am asks his customer to try his product at least sixteen times. In the end, the customer enthusiastically proclaims his love of green eggs and ham and thanks Sam-I-Am. Imagine Sam-I-Am working for your cause, telling your audience there is something specific they can do, an action as specific as *Try this meal!* His focus on that one step is relentless. You may not have the funds to get your message to your audience sixteen times so you have to make each impression count.

How do you effectively get the word out and make it count? One way is to make that impression unforgettable. In *Made to Stick*, Chip and Dan Heath tell a story about Art Silverman with the Center for Science in the Public Interest (CSPI), a group that educates the public about nutrition issues. Through lab testing, CSPI had discovered the coconut oil in a medium bag of popcorn at a movie theater contained almost two days' worth of unhealthy saturated fat. Silverman knew that people wouldn't avoid the popcorn because of a message about "37 grams of saturated fat." It was mind-numbingly scientific. So he brought the data to life in a press conference with a message as described by the Heath brothers, "A medium-sized 'butter' popcorn at a typical neighborhood movie theatre contains more artery-clogging fat than a bacon-and-eggs breakfast, a Big Mac and fries for lunch, and a steak dinner with all the trimmings—combined!"[48] And the props were "the full buffet of greasy food for the television cameras. An entire day's worth of unhealthy eating, displayed on a table. All that saturated fat— stuffed into a single bag of popcorn."

The story took off and found its way into the national networks, newspapers, magazines, and late-night talk shows with headlines like "Theatre Popcorn is Double Feature of Fat." It didn't take long for the theatres to switch from coconut oil. In their book, the Heath brothers point to six elements that help make a message "sticky." They form the acronym SUCCES:

Simple. Find the core idea and share it.

Unexpected. Grab and hold people's attention through surprise.

Concrete. Make the abstract real to help people understand and remember.

Credible. Help people believe. Use details, compelling statistics, and examples.

Emotional. Make people care about the idea.

Stories. Use stories to inspire people to action.

Whether reaching out online or sending a fundraising letter, your audience is busy and the background noise is loud. You want your message to be heard, to stick. You may have to get creative. Yarn-bombers tie scarves around trees in urban centers and parks to draw attention to homelessness and provide warmth to unsheltered folks on cold winter streets. Nineteen-sixties anti-war activists burned draft cards. National Football League player Colin Kaepernick kneeled during the national anthem to protest police brutality and racial inequality in the United States.

In the early eighties, the mysterious retrovirus AIDS began showing up in the United States. It particularly hit gay men, IV drug users, and those who'd had blood transfusions, such as hemophiliacs. In a just a few years AIDS grew to pandemic level, yet many accused the Reagan administration of ignoring the issue due to homophobia. Gay activists and others wondered how to bring this crisis the attention it needed. One such person was Cleve Jones. In 1985, Jones was stapling posters on San Francisco walls and telephone poles to promote the upcoming annual candlelight march and memorial service for Harvey Milk and George Moscone. In an interview for *Xtra Magazine*, he tells of noticing a newspaper headline announcing that a thousand San Franciscans had already died of AIDS. There at the corner of Castro and Market he realized that "almost every one of them had lived and died within six blocks of where I was standing." Jones was frustrated that the suffering and death were invisible. But he had plenty of poster boards and markers, so he asked people at the march to write the names of people they knew who had died. Then using ladders, they taped the posters on the San Francisco Federal Building. When Jones looked at it, it reminded him of a quilt.

> And when I said *quilt* to myself, I thought of my grandma and my great-grandma, and it seemed like such a middle-American family values traditional sort of symbol. And I thought, what a perfect symbol to attach to this disease that's killing homosexuals and African Americans and IV drug users. Everybody told me it was the stupidest thing they had heard of. It was so nerve-racking. I could just see it in my head so clearly how it would look stretched out on the [national] mall, covering the mall. And I could see how it could work as therapy for people who were grieving, as a tool for the media to understand the lives that were behind the statistics, as a weapon to shame the government for its inaction. And everybody saying it was really dumb. I always tell young people if you have an idea that you know in your heart you have to do and everybody tells you it totally sucks, just ignore them and do it![49]

That year, Jones made the first panel in memory of a friend and invited others to create patches. In 1987 they moved the AIDS memorial quilt to the mall of the nation's Capital. The giant quilt with 1,920 panels covered two city blocks. In a somber event it was unveiled section-by-section as volunteers read the name of each person who had died—Clayton Berry, Raymond Case, Dave Castro. Parents, siblings, friends, partners, and others hugged and cried. Millions saw the images on television and in their newspapers. The acres of quilt patches said to the world that those who died from AIDS were not statistics but individuals, loved and remembered. The moment personalized AIDS and helped shift America's will to take greater action. Today, with 48,000 panels representing 80,000 people, the quilt still resonates…and raises awareness.

Call us to action

Communication campaigns are not meant to inform or entertain (although many do both), but ultimately, to get people to do something. And messaging is developed around the action you want the audience to take. Lay out the problem and then present the solution showing how it makes a better world. A call to action asks the audience to help make that solution happen. Whether it's on your home page or a talk to the local civic club, it is the end point of your appeal and the beginning of action toward the better future. Here are a few suggestions for a strong call to action:

- **Suggest specific acts.** You have laid out a problem and a solution; now give folks a specific way to help, something you could actually see them do. *Please call today!* Polite and clear. Donate by clicking here, sign this petition, join this march, wear a pink ribbon. These give your audience a real way to get involved with your cause. Homegrown National Park asks "homeowners, property owners, land managers, farmers, and anyone with some soil to plant in to start a new habitat by planting native plants and removing most invasive plants." These folks with soil are also told that they can help reach a Big Hairy Audacious Goal: "This is the largest cooperative conservation project ever conceived or attempted."

- **Focus on the one thing you need.** Since 1971 when President Nixon ended the draft, the United States has depended on people to volunteer for its armed forces. Young men and women are being asked to risk their lives for their country. A video on the U.S. Army website beckons, "Join the team that makes a difference." "It's your job to solve the world's greatest challenges." The messaging continues with incentives: *Earn a bonus up to $40,000.* The Army wants that potential recruit to connect with them so they can begin the conversation. The site is covered with *Email us, Call us,* and clickable buttons: *See what it takes. Apply online.* What they really want is that live lead, for that someone who might be interested to contact them. Be concise. A nonprofit's fundraising letter asks for one singular thing: a donation. It will probably offer a few ways to give: The website is listed for online donations, there's a return envelope for a check, and it includes a toll-free number to call.

- **Make your call to action stand out.** The call to action needs to be obvious. In the visual message—print, online, or a billboard—make it stand out by surrounding it with negative space or giving it larger type or a different color. If it's audio, like a presentation, radio, or stream, repeat it, say it different ways.

- **Right time, right place.** If possible, schedule your call at an actionable moment and place. Many churches know this: They pass the offering plate every time people gather to worship. People showing up at an event are asked at the door if they want to sign the petition or sign up for the e-newsletter. If you're trying to get people to register to vote, the voter registration cards are right there to fill out.

- **Overcome concerns.** What concerns do people have about your group? Address them near the call to action. To grow to more than 100 million subscribers, Netflix assured people they could easily opt out: "Watch anywhere. Cancel anytime."

- **Remove the barriers.** Some asks will be easy, while others are harder: from committing to a weekly volunteer spot to risking arrest for an act of civil disobedience. No matter where your ask is on that spectrum, remove as many barriers as you can. Make the path as smooth as possible for your supporter's journey. On Homegrown National Park's home page, in big all-caps are the words *PLANT NATIVE*, "no experience necessary, start digging and get on the map!" And for those wondering where to get these native plants, just below these words is a big button—*Find Native Plants in Your Area*—that links you with a growing list of local providers.

In *Certain Trumpets*,[50] Garry Wills explores the partnership between leaders and followers. He says that for there to be leadership there have to be people willing to follow toward the agreed-upon goal. Without them, says Wills, "The best ideas, the strongest will, the most wonderful smile have no effect."

> When Shakespeare's Welsh seer Owne Glendower boasts that "I can call spirits from the vasty deep," Hotspur deflates him with the commonsense answer: "Why, so can I, or so can anyone. But will they come when you do call them?" It is not the noblest call that gets answered, but the *answerable* call.

Wills says Abraham Lincoln didn't have the noblest vision of human equality in his day; the abolitionists did. But his career was developed mutually between his leadership and the followers' "say" in where they were being led. "A leader who neglects that fact soon finds himself without followers. To sound a certain trumpet does not mean just trumpeting one's own certitudes. It means sounding a specific call to specific people capable of response." A good call to action tells people how they can help make the world better and takes into account where they are now and where they are willing to go.

Bring us in with a story

Ray White's 30-year journalism career and passion for the cause made him a great, though unassuming, leader of public relations much of the time I was at Heifer International. While the team was small—Ray, an associate, and some help from a two-person agency—their work yielded fantastic publicity year after year. One day Ray told me "We want to reach out to Nicholas Kristof. He's the most likely to understand what we're doing. Let's see if we can get his attention." A Pulitzer Prize-winning author and highly respected *New York Times* columnist, Kristof had been covering poverty and international issues, often from war zones and places of desperate poverty like Sudan, with a distinct bias toward real, on-the-ground people. Well, it turns out that everybody and their dog was also trying to get his attention. So, how was that going to happen?

Ray knew that journalists like to tell stories that also relate political and social narratives. He called Kristof's assistant, Winter Miller, and gave her the brief Heifer spiel. And the next time he went to New York, he arranged to meet with her in the company cafeteria. "She became more and more interested as we talked because Heifer's program is unlike anything else," Ray told me. "A cow or a goat is a wonderful thing to give to someone because it can reproduce and that means that the person who gets the animal can pass on a gift of another animal like they got to someone else. So it spreads throughout the community." That meeting with the assistant paid off. One day Ray heard from Kristof that he was interested. They emailed back and forth for a while and then Kristof let Ray know he was giving a speech in Dallas and invited him to meet. They met at his hotel after the speech. In July 2008, Kristoff ran a column about a Heifer program recipient in Uganda, a girl named Beatrice whose family had received the gift of some goats that enabled her to go to school—and changed her life. She had been featured in a Heifer video. How long did it take for Ray to meet his goal of connecting Kristof with the Heifer story? Three years. You never know where an intention will lead. You may get there, you may not. The key is to set an intention…and go for it. In 1991, Jo Luck, then head of Heifer International, was sitting in a circle of women in a remote Zimbabwe village. She asked each to share the answer to this question, "What are your dreams for the future?" When it came to her turn, a woman named Tererai said, "I'm a poor woman living in Africa, I've got five kids, I can't have a dream." Jo Luck pressed and asked, "If you *could* have a dream what would it be?" Tererai responded: to get an education. So, Jo Luck answered back, *"If you believe in your dreams, they are achievable." Tinogona* means "It is achievable." Tererai had grown up in a poor cattle-herding family and was married off as an eleven-year-old girl. But she had taught herself to read. Now with *tinogona* as her watchword, she decided that her dreams were to study in the United States, get a bachelor's degree, then a master's, and finally, a Ph.D. She wrote a check list that she wrapped in plastic, placed in a can, and buried under a rock. Tererai began by working on her elementary school education. Then she got a GRE certificate. This determined woman attracted the attention of the Heifer staff in her area. She was encouraged to go further and got a scholarship to go to Oklahoma State University. Her mother sold a cow and other villagers sold small livestock to help send Tererai and her family to the United States. Once there, it never came easy. She was at times so destitute that she resorted to getting food from the trash. Some kind people in the university community rallied to help her. Tererai pressed on and earned her bachelor's degree. And then her master's. And finally, she began working on her Ph.D. at Western Michigan University. Meanwhile, she ended up working at Heifer's head-quarters in Little Rock, where I got to know her.

Then Ray White's gentle persistence paid off. Again. He had been telling columnist Nicholas Kristof about Tererai. In 2009,

Kristof wrote a second column on Heifer, this time about this remarkable woman. It began, "Any time anyone tells you that a dream is impossible, any time you're discouraged by impossible challenges, just mutter this mantra: Tererai Trent." Of course, he set her story in the context of global priorities:

> Tererai is a reminder of the adage that talent is universal, while opportunity is not. There are still 75 million children who are not attending primary school around the world. We could educate them all for far less than the cost of the proposed military "surge" in Afghanistan.

> Each time Tererai accomplished one of those goals that she had written long ago, she checked it off on that old, worn paper. Last month, she ticked off the very last goal, after successfully defending her dissertation. She'll receive her Ph.D. next month, and so, a one-time impoverished cattle-herder from Zimbabwe with less than a year of elementary school education will don academic robes and become Dr. Tererai Trent.[51]

Later, Kristof and his wife Sheryl WuDunn included her story in their book *Half the Sky*.

One day, Ray got a call from a producer of the Oprah Winfrey show. Now, Heifer had already been featured on the show a couple of times, but the piece in *Half the Sky* had captured their attention again, and the producer told Ray they were interested in doing Tererai's story. "They were actually willing to send a crew to Africa," recalled Ray, "which is pretty unusual. Daytime shows don't send crews anywhere." They were soon all off to Zimbabwe. "We're driving up near the Zambezi River to shoot the story in three or four vehicles because they carry a lot of equipment," Ray told me. "We stopped in a field near the village and we heard drums announcing our arrival." They pulled into the village and met everybody, including Tererai's mother, a true supporter and encourager. The show aired in 2009. "It was a great story," he said.

So great that in 2011, when Oprah hosted her final show, she invited Tererai and named her the "all-time favorite guest." Tererai spoke of the unbelievable feeling of walking across the stage to receive her doctorate. When Oprah asked of her current dream, Tererai expressed the need to give back to the millions of girls not getting an education so they don't have to go through what she did. At that point, Oprah announced that she was donating $1.5 million so Tererai could rebuild her childhood elementary school in northern Zimbabwe. Today, through the organization founded by Dr. Tererai Trent, along with Save the Children, more than five thousand children have received education from eleven schools. Tererai says she's just getting started.

This circuitous story is about of a lot of remarkable people, each finding their own way to move us toward life. It's about a leader (my boss for almost two decades) who found it vital to sit in a circle with women most would overlook and to ask what's important in their lives. It's about an affable and persistent PR guy who gave a damn and also knew the importance of stories. It's about journalists, truth-tellers who do their best to shine a light on the real world, including a cultural and media icon who has spent her remarkable career and celebrity lifting up others. And it's about the countless groups and individuals who helped and encouraged in so many ways along the way. All of their lives brushed up against improbability. Finally, it's about a woman who believed when she was assured *It is achievable!*, and is now passing on the gift by infusing *tinogona* into thousands of young people in her own northern Zimbabwe.

Storytelling is an ancient art for a reason: Stories are powerful when they speak to our emotions and can resonate for generations. Ray White knows their power. So do Nicholas Kristof and Oprah Winfrey, who built their careers around sharing stories. While the stories of your cause will not land you as Oprah's all-time favorite guest—that's already happened—they can move the rest of us to support you and your cause. Successful businesses often have a great story to tell: a high-tech company starts with a couple of geeks tinkering in a suburban garage, here's what happened... The same is true for nonprofits. Heifer International began when volunteer Dan West, an Indiana farmer, was handing out powdered milk to victims of the Spanish Civil War. He realized that what they needed was not a cup of milk but a cow, so they could have milk every day, but many had lost their animals to the conflict. When he returned to Indiana, he began to talk with other farmers and church members about sending dairy cows to war-torn Europe. Because of the German U-boats, the first ship loaded with heifers had to go instead to struggling families in Puerto Rico. After the war, "sea-going cowboys" (and a few "sea-going cowgirls") accompanied ships to provide thousands of dairy cows and other livestock to war-torn Europe and Japan.

Stories can take us to the Titanic on that fateful night or on a mission to Mars. They let us imagine life as a rabbit in a hillside warren. The characters face dilemmas, conflict, and trouble; they stumble, fail, and succeed just like we do. Stories shape us, both as individuals and collectively. Few people want to be told how to think or what to do, but we're all open to hearing stories. The stories can open a channel that allows us to hear a new message. So, where do you want to take your audience? How did your story begin? Who are your heroes? What happened in their life? As you weave your stories into the larger narrative you invite your audience to journey with you.

By their nature, statistics are usually boring. But occasionally a surprising statistic can help build a powerful story. It was a statistic—the combined lawn of the United States adding up to 40 million acres, the size of New England—that helped move Doug Tallamy to start Homegrown National Park. And remember the statistic about 37 grams of "artery-clogging fat" in movie-goers popcorn? The greasy-food buffet presentation got theatre owners to quickly switch to less harmful popcorn oil. Presented creatively and compellingly, your cause can also use jarring facts to attract support.

Naming and framing for change

"All big changes of the world come from words."
—Marjane Satrapi

Like a magician's incantation, carefully chosen words can have spell-casting power and help us improve the world. Words evoke powers in different ways. Some phrases call us to take a certain action, *live off-grid*, have a *designated driver*, or to join a protest movement using *nonviolence*. Other phrases simply describe, like *old-growth forest* or *endangered species*. Case-in-point: In recent years almost one-third of our bee colonies have disappeared due to pesticides and habitat loss. This loss seriously threatens our ability to grow enough food, and many now argue that the bumblebee be considered for endangered species status. This vanishing bee crisis has helped spread a new vocabulary including *colony collapse disorder, backyard pollinators, urban apiary, raw honey*. The terms reflect challenges and solutions, practices and products. Just reading this list might cause you to wonder if you should act differently about honey or even consider putting a bee hive in your yard. With words, we can imagine new ways to do things, help people see more clearly, and spread a good practice. Thoughtful language can help determine the future.

Describing new possibilities. How can vocabulary change behavior? Filmmaker, artist, and photographer Douglas Gayeton's book *Local* is about new ways of farming in America. But it's just as much about the power of words, of naming. A new practice starts somewhere. It's then shared among neighbors, at conferences, in blogs or books. The concept begins to take root in more and more people's minds. Someone along the way gives it a name that sticks: *slow food, cage-free eggs, fallen fruit, foodshed, food miles*. The practice of being a *locavore* (eating locally) often spreads once the term—and its implications—is understood. Gayeton says that change means learning a new language. "It all begins with words. By learning the words of this new language—the lexicon—you can start the conversation, even embrace ideas that had previously seemed foreign or irrelevant to your daily life. If you start by learning what the term *food miles* means, for example, the transformation begins."[52] Movements usually create their own unique practices and vocabulary. The nineteenth century effort to end slavery became known as *abolitionism*—don't waste time talking about how to improve this wicked system, completely abolish it! In the United States, it generated the *underground railroad*, a hidden network of routes slaves used to escape to Canada. Secret *safe houses* and meeting places called *stations* and *depots* were managed by *station masters. Conductors*, such as Harriet Tubman, guided escaped slaves along the routes. The term *underground railroad* both evoked one way to deal with a social challenge and reflected a real practice.

Language frames the conversation. Many of our political battles are really highly-strategized language wars. What something is called influences how we perceive it. Is that billionaire a *job creator* who needs to be unfettered from taxes to help the economy, or a *one-percenter* whose money controls too many politicians, persuading them to work against the people who elected them? Was the controversial Keystone pipeline a *job creator* and the answer to U.S. unemployment? Or would it create only thirty-five permanent jobs and is really how a few *one-percenters* could move *dirty fossil fuels* from Canada to the Gulf Coast to sell for export? The gay marriage debate shifted when it was re-framed as *marriage equality*. How about abortion? Are you opposed to taking an innocent life and are *pro-life*? Yet so many who are pro-life also oppose nutrition programs for pregnant women and young children, and oppose free preschool and many social support systems needed for a quality life. Many are also pro-death penalty and were at the vanguard against the masks and COVID-19 vaccinations that could have saved hundreds of thousands of lives. *Pro-birth* might be more accurate, some suggest, or *forced birth*. But the pro-life brand it is for now. Or are you *pro-choice*? A woman should not be told what to do with her body and life choices, right? Each side is strategically named and framed, but language will continue to evolve.

Branding and legitimacy. When an action has a catchy name, many others must be doing it, right? So, if you join, you're not alone. With naming you can brand an issue or practice, highlight its importance, and reinforce its legitimacy. The more people hear the phrase, the more it becomes important, something they should consider doing or supporting. *Xeriscaping*, landscaping in a way that reduces or cuts out the need to water, provides an accepted (or even desired) alternative to traditional yards. Perfectly uniform grass lawns depend on fertilizer, pesticides, and plenty of water. *No-mow* offers another alternative. When practices have names, like *xeriscaping, rewilding,* and *no-mow* (or at least *no-mow* May), they become normalized, more legitimate. Add to that whole books and websites about them indicating, obviously, other people are onboard, and we have more courage to try a new practice ourselves.

Exposing wrong. Language can raise questions about "business as usual." It can also bring to light a bad practice. A term like *fair trade* implies an opposite: other coffees may somehow be unfair to the farmer. *Equal rights* implies a society where some folk's rights are less than others'. Some police officers pull people over or stop them on the sidewalk merely for looking "wrong," often for the color of their skin: *profiling*. *Apartheid*, the South African system of racial segregation, is Afrikaans for *apart-hood*. The anti-apartheid movement was able to globally brand apartheid as the horrific system it was. Through the power of words, practices that would have otherwise gone unnoticed are exposed. *Ghost fishing* was first brought to the world's attention in the 1980s. It's what happens when nets, abandoned by commercial fishers, continue to trap and kill fish, sea turtles, and marine mammals. Naming the problem is a key step in solving it.

Create new paths for society. Sometimes a new lexicon creates and reflects a new approach to an entire aspect of society. The food movement, with its dozens of new phrases, reflects a shift away from the dominant corporate processed food model and towards a system that is friendly to people and the environment, not to mention our own health. In reclaiming our once abandoned city centers, the *New Urbanism* movement has spawned *walkable neighborhoods* that attract new residents and shops and transform an area. The movement has also spawned a giant lexicon: *bike paths, buffered bike lanes, walkability, pocket parks, pedestrian continuity, placemaking*, and so on. A *sharrow*, for example, is the name of a road marking consisting of a painted bike and chevron. It indicates that this road is a priority bicycle route and is shared by both cars and bikes. The hope is to get cars to be better prepared to share and to encourage cyclists to go the right way in the lane. Since the symbol's introduction in San Francisco in 2004, it has spread throughout U.S. cities.

Consumer choice. In the grocery store you face a colorful shelf of coffee bags. Labels on some say *Organic* or *Fair Trade Certified*. They cost a bit more but they could be healthier for the planet and allow us to directly help the struggling farmers who grew the beans. I once sat with a group of coffee growers in Guatemala as they listed about twenty ways being able to sell organic, fair trade coffee transformed their families' lives. I was surprised at how important the shift was for them. For example, they were no longer sick from pesticides, they weren't polluting the lake downstream (which improved fishing), and the extra money helped them send their children to school. These new lexicons invite us to shop differently. Our everyday choices give us power to create the world we would like to live in. We can *boycott* a company or store that discriminates against people or funds efforts we don't like. And we can *procott* (intentionally buy things) businesses that do things we agree with. When we *buy local*, our dollars stay in our communities (instead of going to distant shareholders' pockets) to fund our neighborhood schools and roads and grow the local economy. We vote for the future of the world with our dollars.

"The difference between the almost right word and the right word is really a large matter," said Mark Twain. "It's the difference between the lightning bug and the lightning." Pay attention to the ever-changing lexicons that help us make better choices and use the power of language to boost your cause. Each of us has a unique voice that the world needs. Tell your stories, present your case, call us to action through books, online articles, speeches, songs, poetry, plays, television, movies, and blogs. Your words can change the world!

CHAPTER SEVEN

Brands, names, and symbols

A story is going around about a rat and hamster relaxing by the backyard pool. The rat asks the hamster, "What gives? We're about the same, yet the family here loves you. They think you're cute. They've given you a nice home and bring you food every day. Meanwhile, I'm out here in the rain struggling to survive. People hate me, think I'm disgusting, and try to kill me. What's the difference?" The hamster responds: "It's just branding." Businesses like Starbucks, Nike, and Disney, and celebrities like Oprah, Jennifer Lopez, and Elon Musk have mastered the power of the brand. Of course, Donald Trump leveraged his unique brand all the way into the White House. Effective branding can take a business or person to a new level. It can also help transform your cause. Yes, the brand is the logo. But it's also the name, design, color, font. And it's your website, printed materials, the music introducing your podcast, how you are portrayed in the media. It's how supporters talk about you to their friends. It's how people see you in a hundred ways, their entire experience of your organization. It's everything a customer or supporter feels about you and your products and services. Your brand should tell a story, create buzz, excite people, and let them know how they can help.

It's up to you to create and manage the brand so it works in your favor. And it's worth obsessing over!

Why does your brand matter? Your cause depends on your key supporters. Every day, literally thousands of messages fight for the attention of the person you want to reach. How do you get through the clutter? How do you emotionally connect with that potential partner? An established, positive brand serves as a short-cut. Like the aroma of bread baking in the oven, your brand can signal to your supporter a good feeling and help them focus on your message.

Define your brand—what makes you unique? Start with a clear brand identity or position. What's your organization's essence? What are you doing that people want? What's your niche? If you're not different, why should anyone care about you? To define your brand, you've got to be able to answer these questions. The Grateful Dead is famous for its brand identity. In *Strategy + Business*,[53] New York Times technology writer Glenn Rifkin says the band "managed to hold on to its special perch in the fickle world of entertainment for more than 30 years, becoming a gold standard in an industry that has seen thousands of other rock 'brands' come and go." Some things the Grateful Dead got right: They knew their customers; they filled a need of that customer; they created (and stayed with) a community, building great trust with their followers; and they focused on quality, making sure the experience was always great. Jerry Garcia said, "You do not merely want to be considered just the best of the best. You want to be considered the only ones who do what you do." Keep your brand simple, singular. Can you create a new category, something only you do, and focus on that? Find a way to stand out, preferably related to how you operate. Girl Scouts send a couple million kids out to sell cookies, the hammer-wielding volunteer brands Habitat for Humanity, while Greenpeace fights high-drama battles against environment-destroying Goliaths.

Multiple audiences. Your brand is important to more than just your supporters. In its rebranding journey, MD Anderson Cancer Center noted that they wanted to reach several audiences. "Brand drives about a third of choice decisions for three stakeholder groups: for patients' decisions to seek treatment at MD Anderson; for physicians' decisions to refer to MD Anderson, and for potential employees' decisions to apply to MD Anderson. It is a crucial influencer of employees' decisions to remain at MD Anderson."[54]

Be real. You typically don't have a serious relationship with someone you just met, it takes time to know each other, learn whether they're trustworthy, fun, and authentic. Likewise, your group's relationship with a supporter may take years to mature. Your brand has to be authentic. Be what you say you are, practice what you preach, be transparent. And be relevant to your supporters: Do something they want done.

Beyond your control. While you can do plenty to define your brand, you can't completely control it. Through the news, social media, even word of mouth, the public can also define your brand. Facebook comments, blog posts, and news articles (positive or negative) can also drive the conversation. In 2012, when the Susan G. Komen Race for the Cure announced that they would no longer support cancer screening/prevention programs at Planned Parenthood, their brand took a giant hit from the firestorm of criticism that followed. The group quickly reversed course, but many wondered if they could recover. Years and other controversies later, the Komen brand still carries for millions a positive emotional power. When you hit a setback, simply get up, learn the lessons, and get moving again. Brands are built over years.

Once you've developed your brand identity, let it permeate every object, every event, every message. You may even get tired of it, but you're not the main audience. Your now and future supporters are.

The Heifer International re-brand

In the 1940s, *Heifers for Relief* began by sending ships full of dairy cows and other farm animals to the countries devastated by World War II. Early on it was renamed *Heifer Project International*. For almost two decades, I led Heifer's marketing and communications. When I started in 1992, Heifer was almost fifty years old. The organization was much smaller than many similar organizations its age. In those early days, I had on my desk a "brand" folder where I gathered materials printed by offices around world. In a short time, I had collected more than fifty different variations of the Heifer's logo and logotype treatment. Most had a globe with longitude and latitude lines. They usually had five or six (but not always the same) animals. Peru's logo had llamas. Some logos added people or trees. The logotype was all over the place, with many fonts, colors, size variations, and different words. Some used all caps and some just used *HPI*. In short, the brand was random, confusing, and ineffective. It was time to rebrand, including the logo and maybe even the name. I also had on my desk a directory of international humanitarian organizations. Along with the descriptions and contact information of the 160 groups were their logos. One day in a few minutes of research and analysis (okay, I was just counting), I discovered that when you eliminated the logos with these four art elements— globes, hands, wheat and stylized human figures with outstretched arms—only about ten were left! One hundred fifty organizations were using some version of just four images! A good logo is simple, singular, and unique. And you should recognize it even though it's in the background of a photo and blurred. Heifer had an opportunity to stand out from the crowd.

We asked Girvin Design of Seattle to lead us through a branding program. They had almost no nonprofit experience (they'd just finished the Bellagio in Las Vegas) but something about them seemed right. They seemed to get us and were motivated to help, they didn't see it as another job. Wanting the process to be participatory, in eight different sessions starting in 1999, we gathered input, got reactions to images, concepts, words, and values from literally hundreds of volunteers, staff (including leaders from more than forty countries), board members, and others. Each time we met, the Girvin team helped us focus just a bit more. From these sessions Girvin developed a Brand Positioning Statement that emphasized self-reliance for families and sustainability. We also developed the elements of the Brand Personality such as *visionary* and *reliable*. Then we developed a short list of Desired Brand Perceptions that included *holistic solutions* and *rich legacy*.

Now it was time to look at the logo. Creating a logo by committee is like writing by committee, except much worse! It turns out that people can be passionate about what symbols represent them. Everyone wanted their pet issue represented: besides a variety of animals (*goats are most important!*), we had to include people because that's who we help, and a house that represents community, and a tree for the environment. And a sun that represented something that I can't even remember. After many months, we had a logo with about six elements. It sucked. One day, in a short phone call I asked the Girvin team leader for a full design treatment that cut out everything but the one cow. They sent it, we showed it around, and that became our logo!

And the name, did we want to change it altogether? It was quickly agreed that *HPI* was cold and didn't inspire our desired brand personality. The word *Heifer* had challenges. Few people know what one is (a young cow that hasn't yet had a calf), it's also used as a derogatory insult. But we recognized that we already had a lot of equity in the word *Heifer*. With millions of impressions out there, for many it perfectly summarized our effort. After several sessions, we decided to keep Heifer and to make the word mean us. "International" was kept to show the depth and breadth of the organization. It would be in smaller type to emphasize Heifer.

"Project" had no value and even implied that our work was temporary, so after six decades, we dropped it.

Heifer International...

Looking back, it seems like a lot of work to just drop one superfluous word. But it was a process we had to go through. Now we had a new logo and a slightly different name. We developed a brand guidebook—a tool kit with rules for colors, fonts, and different uses—and we sent it to Heifer offices around the world. Now it was time for the roll-out.

Remember that we had gone to great lengths over the course of two years to include the country programs in the process? When we put the new branding guidelines out there, we immediately heard that the leaders who worked with U.S. farmers didn't like it and wouldn't use it. "It's too whimsical!" In the country where we had to raise tens of millions of dollars each year, having two brands would be a disaster. And from a few other countries came, "We don't like it! No one will know who we are." The African program had branded Heifer as "HPI." It was on all their printed materials, their offices, vehicles, and thousands of t-shirts and caps worn by partner farmers. Several countries simply refused to use the new logo and branding guidelines. After a few months of this, Heifer's president finally told them that they were free to keep their old looks, but any program that did would no longer get funds from headquarters. Soon the new brand was universally adopted! After all the bluster, the switch turned out to be a non-event.

And a few naysayers warned that donations would dry up because people were so tied to the old globe logo and the word *project*. Instead, that first year we mailed materials to millions of supporters using Heifer International along with the new logo, we did great. During the process we also created name consistency for the country programs. That actually went well. There was a nice ring to Heifer Uganda, Heifer China, Heifer Poland and so on. In later battles, we brought the names of other assets into alignment.

For example, the International Learning and Livestock Center in Arkansas (informally called "the ranch") became Heifer Ranch. As passions come into play, what should have taken months took two years. With patience, Girvin stuck with us, didn't charge any more for all the extra time, and stayed positive.

But once we switched, it didn't take long for the old logos and names to disappear, even from our consciousness. We had moved on. If you were to see the "leaping cow" at a distance or quickly (for example, it appeared on a coffee mug for two seconds in an episode of the popular TV show The Office) you would recognize it. It's unique. No other nonprofit has anything like it. Heifer went from relatively unknown to one of the top recognized organizations working to end poverty. These increases are not just because of rebranding; we were mailing millions of gift catalogs every year. We had celebrity support, lots of PR, and thousands of congregations and schools were adopting our programs. Was the process messy? Absolutely! But we ended up with a strong brand that helped Heifer make more cost-effective impressions to raise funds and public awareness. With a coordinated branding effort, your group will be better poised to attract new supporters and deepen the connection with existing ones.

Experience the brand

Quit reading now and take a minute to think of an actual place that means a great deal to you—where you are energized or nourished. Is there a park, a certain neighborhood or street, a section along a river?

Hey, you're still reading! Really, stop and think of that place. How do you experience it? What makes it special?

When it comes to branding, it helps to think of an organization as a place we all experience. When you visit your group's "place," will you feel like you're in a dark alley, not wanting to go further? Or on that traffic-choked street lined with fast-food restaurants, strip malls, and power lines? Or hopefully, will you feel like you're going down a tree-lined country lane, relaxing in a garden, or sitting in a coffee shop full of people talking and connecting with each other? "Brand" used to mean logo, typeface, color, packaging, jingles, and ads. Today it's better thought of as the overall experience anyone—a supporter, customer, passerby—has when they brush against your organization. Each year thousands, if not millions, will come into contact with your group. They may catch sixty seconds on the local news, see a magazine article, or view a friend's Facebook Like. They may glimpse it on a website or t-shirt, or talk with a staff person or volunteer. The cumulative effect of these visits forms the experience that person has of your organization. Whether they sought you out or stumbled upon you, they will judge you; if the experience is bad or mediocre, an opportunity is lost. But if it's positive—if it moves the person toward confidence and loyalty—you may gain a lifetime friend. What difference does place make? How we experience place matters. The spaces we occupy can pull us down or lift us up. Some workplaces are brutal to the souls who toil there day after day, while other spaces give us a boost. Plenty of studies have shown how people feel better, relate better, and are more productive when working in natural light or around nature. Some spaces are neatly organized, while others offer more creative chaos. The wild array of beauty in nature or in our human-made spaces can inspire us and help us live more fully. What's your nonprofit brand? When someone comes to your place, what do they experience? Do they want to linger and come back?

What's in a name?

Chances are that at some point you'll have created something that needs a name. I've helped name nonprofits, programs, campaigns, and books, plus plenty of pets and two boys—never alone. You probably have also had to come up with a number of names. Each time you want to get it right; it's fun but not always easy. In *Old Possum's Book of Practical Cats*,[55] T.S. Eliot tells us that cats have three names. The first, he says, is the sensible everyday one the family uses: Peter, George. Electra. The second is more particular, dignified: Jellylorum, Bombalurina. The third, the "deep and inscrutable singular name," only the cat knows and won't confess. At Heifer International, we had several names. The family (staff, volunteers, fans) called it *Heifer*. We encouraged that; it was short and easy. The second (official) name, *Heifer Project International, Inc.*, stemmed from its history and gets used in legal documents. The third—unknown to any single person—was our essence, our brand. To name nonprofits, campaigns and programs should think about the three parts:

1. **Common Name:** This is the one to get as right as you can. It's what you want everyone to call your organization or program. It's what appears in the news, on your materials. It has to work.

2. **Official Name:** If you're naming an organization, you'll need this for legal purposes. It's best if it's the same as the common name, but if that doesn't work, it should tie closely to it. (Some states have specific requirements.)

3. **Brand:** While most important, it's beyond the naming process and is, in Eliot's words, "the name that no human research can discover." It's the feeling people have about your organization or program. You can and should *try* to describe it, but it's also indescribable. It's the Essence.

Hunt, gather, murder

A great name can give your cause a giant boost for branding and marketing—adding to your success for years to come. The focus here is on the first, the common name you want people to call you. In step one, you are the hunter/gatherers. Get a bunch of people involved. Make big lists of all kinds of names. Have fun. Tell friends and co-workers what you're up to and encourage everyone to make suggestions. Offer a free lunch for the person who comes up with the winning name. Use libations or mind-altering substances if that's what it takes. But be free and loose. Gather all the names you can.

The second step involves the murders. After a while, you should have a pile of possibilities, so hear the advice of Sir Arthur Quiller-Couch: "Whenever you feel an impulse to perpetrate a piece of exceptionally fine writing, obey it–whole-heartedly–and delete it before sending your manuscripts to press. Murder your darlings." Faulkner later called this heavy editing "Kill your darlings." Whatever you call it, there's no time for all of your name options to die natural deaths. You'll have to murder or kill them all—except one. And that's the name.

Strunk and White's 14th rule in *The Elements of Style* is to "avoid fancy words... Do not be tempted by a twenty-dollar word when there is a ten-center handy, ready and able." Why use *utilize* when you can use *use*, or *purchase* if you mean *buy*? Stephen King says that looking for longer, dressier words is "like dressing up a household pet in evening clothes. The pet is embarrassed and the person who committed this act of premeditated cuteness should be even more embarrassed."[56] Abstract or Latin-based words may not be your friends either. Try to find a name people won't forget.

When you come up with one you like, you can check instantly to see if a domain name is available. You should also check online with the U.S. trademark office for any conflicts. At some point, you may want to hire a lawyer to help you register. Once you've picked it, let it seep for a while. During this time, don't ask people whether they like it or, God forbid, turn the naming process into a vote! Instead, tell some folks about the organization or program using the name as though it were decided. And watch for the reactions—from them and most important, from your own inner voice. At the end of the process, you should feel good about your choice of a nonprofit name or program. (If not, go back to the drawing board!) Then you launch it! When you name cats, nonprofits, kids, and companies, it feels awkward for a short while. Then the name takes, and soon you can't imagine it any other way.

Why do symbols matter?

During the heated debate surrounding Supreme Court nominee Brett Kavanaugh, supporters of a woman's right to choose sent 3,000 coat hangers to the office of Senator Susan Collins. They feared that her *Yes* vote and his confirmation would tip the scales against Roe v. Wade. The hangers symbolized a time when women without choice sometimes died from coat-hanger and illegal back-alley abortions. Players kneel during the national anthem at a sports game to affirm that Black Lives Matter. The colors blue and yellow are displayed around the world to show support for the people of Ukraine during a time of war. Symbols are all around us—in flags, street names, statues, money, images, objects, and acts. They are not there by accident. Someone put them there to change our point of view, misinform, create fear and oppression, recruit and rally supporters, or evoke hope and courage. Symbolic action can never replace real-life action. Nevertheless, mastering the art of symbols can boost your cause in the high-stakes battle for support. How is it that a few scribbled lines can evoke deep emotions? Why does a swastika spray-painted on a synagogue wall transmit energy that emboldens a few (even to violence) and alarms many more? But symbols can also be positive and life-giving, and remind us of our best values. Symbols like the dove or the Statue of Liberty inspire and encourage. They're part of our cultural vocabulary. The symbol of your cause can do the same.

The ever-shifting landscape of symbols often signals who is in power in a given arena and who threatens to overthrow that power. Look no further than the public symbols of the Confederacy in the United States, disturbing reminders that Jim Crow is still alive and well today. The Southern Poverty Law Center (SPLC) has mapped 1,740 of them scattered across the nation, but mostly in the South.[57] These take the form of monuments, place names (such as streets, cities, and counties), schools, and more. For example, the most common person-based street name in Virginia is "Lee,"[58] after the Confederate general. Most of these symbols appeared in two periods: from the 1890s through the 1920s and in the years following the 1954 Brown-vs.-Board of Education Supreme Court decision and Little Rock's Central High School desegregation in 1957. They were and are racist assertions, warnings to not resist White dominance.

In 1961, the Confederate flag was raised in front of the South Carolina state house for the first time in a century. It was, said *Washington Post* columnist Eugene Robinson, "a middle finger directed at the federal government. It was flown there as a symbol of massive resistance to racial desegregation. Period."[59] Such symbols go hand-in-hand with violence. In 2015, a young White man entered an African Methodist Episcopal Church in Charleston, South Carolina and murdered nine members, telling his victims, "You rape our women and you're taking over our country and you have to go." Among the many racist symbols found on his website was the Confederate battle flag. This event prompted responses around the country. The SPLC reports that since that Charleston church shooting, more than a hundred of these public symbols have come down. Ironically, one person who wouldn't have been happy about the proliferation of Confederate symbols was Robert E. Lee himself. It turns out he opposed erecting confederate monuments.[60] "I think it wiser not to keep open the sores of war," said Lee, "but to follow the example of those nations who endeavored to obliterate the marks of civil strife, and to commit to oblivion the feelings it engendered." Symbols of racism and hate should never be welcome and need to be, as Lee urged, committed to oblivion. Instead, Confederate flags wave in abundance today on poles, bumper stickers, and t-shirts. But activists are steadily taking them on, one at a time.

"All the world's a stage," said William Shakespeare. Just as a flag can be a symbol, so can an act. And some have learned the power of creating symbolic actions and moments in our real-world theatre. Think of the everyday founders of our nation at the Boston Tea Party in 1773 to protest unfair taxation without representation, or the November night in 1989 when East and West Germans met and danced on top of the cruelly divisive Berlin wall as it began tumbling down. On a June day in 2015, in an act of civil disobedience at the South Carolina state house, Bree Newsome climbed up the pole of the offending flag that had flown since 1961. She unclipped it and brought it down. "We removed the flag today because we can't wait any longer. We can't continue like this another day," she said. "It's time for a new chapter where we are sincere about dismantling white supremacy and building toward true racial justice and equality."[61] What act in the public good—that lifts up others—can your cause commit?

Journey of the Harriet Tubman Twenty

Even people can become symbols. Hitler and Putin symbolize the worst manifestations of humankind. Others like Lincoln, Elvis, Frida, Einstein, Madonna, and Mother Theresa we call icons. They appear throughout this book like sprinkles on ice cream. We evoke them through quotes and put their images on t-shirts and posters for both inspiration and profit. Images and statues let people *long dead* whisper to us, remind us what they stood for, good or bad. On the front of the penny we see an image of Abraham Lincoln. Even though a coin is small, it's a public space, and the words and images on it belong to all of us. When we pass a few pennies to a cashier, we're probably not thinking about his presidency, but the Lincoln icon and the values of freedom and equality for all that he stood for are unconsciously reinforced. Sometimes, though, we're reinforcing the wrong values. Every time we spend a twenty-dollar bill—at this writing—we see Andrew Jackson, with his large forehead and long wavy hair. He is embraced today by the White far right as a populist hero. President Jackson is known for his key role in a White land grab when he signed the Indian Removal Act that forced Native Americans to leave their ancestral lands in the South and march to current day Oklahoma. In what became known as the Trail of Tears, exposure to the elements, extortion, violence, disease, and starvation caused the deaths of thousands. Cherokees named him "Indian Killer." He was also known for harsh treatment of his own slaves and fought to expand slavery in the west. While Jackson's image takes up a small public space, it's one that's visited by millions every day.

Over the years, many have wanted to replace his image on the twenty—this time with a woman. In 2014, business owner Barbara Ortiz Howard and journalist Susan Ades Stone formed a nonprofit group called Women on 20s, or W20. Their hope was to have a woman on the bill by the year 2020, the centennial of the 19th Amendment that guaranteed women the right to vote. Says the W20:

> Equality may be legislated, but our culture must embrace it in every way for it to become a reality and erase the lines that have been drawn between us. Women On 20s is one small way to join Americans in a big cultural hug and acknowledge that symbols matter—especially the pictures we put on our money. When we have a woman on our bills, we will connect women to their value throughout history, literally validating their abilities and potential through the millions of bills passing from hand-to-hand every day.[62]

The group's initial list of two hundred candidates was winnowed down in several rounds, and in 2015, they asked people to pick one woman from a field of fifteen. The process was designed to encourage a national conversation—from coffee shops and dinner tables to the national media—about which woman was best for the bill. More than 600,000 people voted and Harriet Tubman emerged as the winner. Over the next year W20 increased public support to convince the Treasury Department to, as their website says, "Replace a slave trader with a freed slave and freedom fighter." And after its own deliberations in 2016, the Obama administration announced that Harriet Tubman, a former slave who became a conductor on the underground railroad as well as an activist who fought for women's right to vote, would be the first African American woman on paper currency. Unfortunately, during the four years that Andrew Jackson's portrait hung prominently in Donald Trump's oval office, that president opposed this idea and his treasury secretary stalled the project. The Biden administration has since rebooted it.

An atlas of symbols

Cities. Places also change their names depending on who's in favor. For example, the Russian city of St. Petersburg was founded in 1703 by Tsar Peter the Great. In 1914, at the outset of World War I, the Tsar felt the name sounded too German so it was renamed Petrograd. When revolutionary politician Vladimir Lenin died in 1924, the city became Leningrad. As the Soviet Union broke up, many other cities switched back to pre-Communist names, and in 1991, the Leningrad citizens voted to go back to St. Petersburg. Each change reflected the rule of the day.

Buildings. Across the United States, buildings named for racists are coming under fire, especially college dorms and other buildings, from Duke to Yale, that are named for slaveholders and white supremacists. In 2015, student protests led the University of North Carolina to redub "Saunders Hall" as "Carolina Hall." In 1920, the classroom building had been named for William Saunders, a former Confederate colonel and head of the state's Ku Klux Klan. The students had urged the trustees to rename the building "Hurston Hall" after the Black writer Zora Neale Hurston.[63] In our nation's capital, efforts are stalled in renaming Washington DC's U.S. Russell Senate Office Building. Richard Russell, Jr. was a Georgia governor, senator—and a White supremacist. Many senators and others would like to rename the building after Senator John McCain.

Geographical Features. Ironically, twenty-six of the U.S. states are named for First Peoples (the same lands from which Native Americans were mostly removed). One of those is Alaska, which is Aleut for mainland. For thousands of years in that land, the First Peoples called North America's highest mountain *Denali*, meaning "the high one." In 1917, it was renamed Mt. McKinley after President William McKinley, who had nothing to do with Alaska. In 2015, it once again became Mt. Denali.

Streets and Parks. To the victor go the spoils, and that includes symbols. Spanish general and dictator Francisco Franco was a nationalist who, aided by Hitler, rose to power in 1939. As many as half a million people died in the Spanish Civil War, and after it ended tens of thousands of Franco's enemies were imprisoned or executed. During his decades-long dictatorship, squares and streets across Spain were renamed for nationalist generals. Now most of Franco's supporters are gone, and a 2007 "historical memory" law called for replacing the symbols of their rule. Dozens of streets in Madrid alone are reverting to their pre-Franco era names or are being named after prominent women and others who resisted the brutal regime. So

General Millan Astray Street, named for a ruthless nationalist officer, was changed to *Teacher Justa Freire Street*, after a well-known and beloved teacher.[64] Imagine the difference this makes to a child growing up on that street. Every city I've lived in has a street named for Martin Luther King, Jr. They also all have an Elm Street, but this is immensely different, and it matters. (Now my Homegrown National Park friends would point out that *Elm* streets *do* matter.) Some researchers at Mapbox analyzed seven major cities worldwide and (after eliminating the gender-neutral names) found that only 28 percent were named for women. The findings of this form of sexism came as no surprise. In the Netherlands, an estimated 88 percent of streets are named for men.[65] It's clear that those who named our streets and other symbols haven't historically valued diversity.

From street-name changes to honor diversity and inclusion, to tens of thousands of women marching in knitted pink hats for women's rights, to White House lights colored in the form of a rainbow to celebrate the Supreme Court's making same sex marriage the law of the land, we live in an age of symbols. Whether we put them to good use is up to us. If you are looking to do good in the world, think about the symbols you choose to present and what they *really* stand for, because people—if not history—will judge you by them. It's an awesome and exciting responsibility.

CHAPTER EIGHT

Exploring possibilities

"We continue to learn or we dig a rut and furnish it."
—Stephen King

A recent rover we earthlings sent to explore the next planet over was named by sixth-grader Clara Ma through a contest: *Curiosity*. But it took seven thousand adults and five years to make it happen. The $2.5 billion spacecraft launched from Florida in November 2011 and landed the next August on Mars. Just landing the craft was an amazing engineering feat. A signal from Mars takes fourteen minutes to reach earth, so onboard computers had to do all the work. In a make-or-break entry called "seven minutes of terror," the craft slowed from 13,000 miles per hour to zero. Because anything slightly off would ruin the landing, there was no room for error. As the spacecraft came into the thin atmosphere, it heated up to 1,600 degrees and deployed the largest supersonic parachute ever built. The craft then used its own rockets to slow it even more. And just twenty meters above the surface, to slow it further, Curiosity was lowered using tethers. The landing was successful, and years later Curiosity is still a working lab on wheels, sending images, drilling into the surface, and analyzing rocks and gasses. While it travelled 350 million miles to get to Mars, it has ventured only about thirty miles on the planet, but in that short distance we've learned a great deal. Curiosity has found evidence of ancient riverbeds and lakebeds that tell us water once flowed on the planet. It has identified organic molecules, the building blocks of life. It's found "burps of methane," perhaps a sign of ancient—or recent—life. And we know more about how humans could live on the planet, with more discoveries to come.

You have your great idea, you've developed a plan for launching your world-changing moment, activity, or agency. You've created your mighty message and considered the ins and outs of brand, name, and symbols. Now, how do you discover flywheel improvements or even a breakthrough? You have neither $2.5 billion nor a staff of seven thousand to find new ways to address your cause, but you probably have more resources than you think. Curiosity is active, not passive, and lucky for us, it can be strengthened and built into our habits through deliberate action. And there are many time-tested approaches that boost our chances of success. In this chapter, we'll look at just a few of them. And one of the first steps is forgetting what you think you know. Pre-knowing the answers will doom your chances of discovery. It's not easy to unlearn, but when you abandon your assumptions you open yourself to new possibilities. In *Five Minds for the Future*, psychologist and Harvard professor Howard Gardner says that child prodigies rarely become true creators because from the earliest age they were rewarded "for doing precisely what the adults in their domain were doing." It's hard for them to shift to creativity. "A wit said of Camille Saint Saëns, an aging musical prodigy who never fully realized his early promise: 'He has everything but he lacks inexperience.'" Gardner continues:

> The creator stands out in terms of temperament, personality, and stance. She is perennially dissatisfied with current work, current standards, current questions, current answers. She strikes out in

unfamiliar directions and enjoys—or at least accepts—being different from the pack. When an anomaly arises… she does not shrink from that unexpected wrinkle: indeed, she wants to understand it and to determine whether it constitutes a trivial error, an unrepeatable fluke, or an important but hitherto unknown truth. She is tough-skinned and robust. There is a reason why so many famous creators hated or dropped out of school—they did not like marching to someone else's tune (and, in turn, the authorities disliked their idiosyncratic marching patterns).[66]

New questions, new possibilities

Have you ever been at a meeting where the group has struggled over some issue for hours and then someone says, "Maybe we're not asking the right question." It's a comment to listen for—like opening the windows to the fresh air. Let's make sure our question can take us where we need to go. The "experts" in your field have probably already stated the questions to which you are supposed to find answers. For example, most nonprofit marketers focus on questions like, how do we increase our renewal rate, click-through rate, average gift size? How do we find new donors? Tens of thousands of staff, professionals, and consultants chase answers to the standard questions, which are certainly worth pursuing. But while our brains lean into what we know and what we've seen work, exploring lesser known paths may lead to greater rewards. *What if instead we asked…* The well-articulated question can be the beginning point for breakthrough and a new understanding. Maybe ask how can we expand our program with no more money? Could our program be paid for with a completely different business model? Is there a different way to accomplish the goal? Is our goal really a good one? If we needed ten times the funds in just one year, how would we get it? In *Creativity*, psychologist Mihaly Csikszentmihalyi distinguishes between *presented* and *discovered* problems:

Problems are not all alike in the way they come to a person's attention. Most problems are already formulated; everybody knows what is to be done and only the solution is missing. The person is expected by employers, patrons, or some other external pressure to apply his or her mind to the solution of a puzzle. These are "presented" problems. But there are also situations in which nobody has asked the question yet. Nobody even knows that there is a problem. In this case the creative person identifies both the problem and the solution. Here we have a "discovered" problem. Einstein, among others, believed that the really important breakthroughs in science come as a result of reformulating old problems or discovering new ones, rather than by just solving existing problems.[67]

"The mere formulation of a problem is far more essential than its solution, which may be merely a matter of mathematical or experimental skills," said Albert Einstein. "To raise new questions, new possibilities, to regard old problems from a new angle requires creative imagination and marks real advances in science."

Reframe the ~~problem~~ challenge

Coming up with a great solution to the wrong problem may feel good in the moment but it can send you down a rabbit hole that wastes time and energy. One way to get better solutions is to reframe your challenge. In his *Harvard Business Review*[68] article "Are You Solving the Right Problems?", innovation and problem-solving thought leader Thomas Wedell-Wedellsborg offers helpful ways to approach challenges. He describes the "slow elevator" example in which frustrated tenants complain to a building's owner that the elevator is too slow and they spend a lot of time waiting. Some even threaten to leave. According to Wedell-Wedellsborg, if the frame is "The elevator is too slow," the "solution space" for this is "make the elevator faster." So possible solutions include replacing the elevator, getting a stronger motor, or improving the algorithm. Instead of these costly solutions the building owner installed mirrors next to the elevators. Why? The challenge was reframed from "the elevator is too slow" to "the wait is annoying." This opened an entirely different set of solutions: put up mirrors, play music, install a hand sanitizer.

Wedell-Wedellsborg offers a real-world example: Each year in the United States about 3 million dogs are brought to shelters to be put up for adoption, but more than a million don't find homes. The problem is usually framed as how to get more people to adopt dogs. But Lori Weiss, the founder of Downtown Dog Rescue in Los Angeles, reframed the challenge. "Rather than seek to get more dogs adopted," he writes, "Weiss tries to keep them with their original families so that they never enter shelters in the first place. It turns out that about 30 percent of the dogs that enter a shelter are 'owner surrenders,' deliberately relinquished by their owners." Weiss told him that in many cases the problem was one of poverty: a sudden eviction, inability to pay for a vet fee, how to feed the kids. They see taking their pet to the shelter as the last option. So the staff now ask families who bring in a pet if they'd rather keep it. If so, "the staff member tries to help resolve the problem, drawing on his or her network and knowledge of the system." The families get to keep their dogs and shelter space is freed up for other animals. Moreover, while it costs Downtown Dog Rescue an average of $85 per dog housed and adopted, this approach costs only $60. As we take the time to reframe challenges and look at them from different perspectives, we open more opportunities for innovative and effective solutions.

These reframing techniques can help you see a challenge through different lenses:

- *Flip from the negative to the positive.* Simply shifting a problem to a challenge or opportunity creates a different attitude with very different solutions.

- *Frame-storming.* Instead of starting with brainstorming solutions to a problem, start by exploring different ways to frame the challenge, or what Tina Seelig calls "frame-storming."[69] Group process facilitators know that asking the best questions is key to good outcomes. A brainstorm on how to plan a birthday party will give you a certain set of results, says Seelig. But if you ask, "How do we plan a birthday celebration?" you'll get different kinds of ideas. And asking, "How do we make that day memorable or special?" will create yet another set of ideas.

- *Ask Why?* You think you know what you want to accomplish, but why do you want to do that? Like the annoying toddler, ask why. Then ask why to that answer. Again, and again. As many times as it takes. Many *whys* in, you may land on a better way to approach your challenge.

- *Reframe your big challenge into a set of smaller challenges.* Most important challenges are complex, and trying to solve a big one in one big bite can be overwhelming. Can your challenge be reframed into a number of smaller challenges? In the spirit of kaizen (small incremental improvements), ask, what are a bunch of small things that can happen to move you toward the goal? Often, groups can list small solutions that could be put into practice immediately without getting anyone's permission.

- *Think of limitations as aids to creativity.* Innovators are almost always underfunded relative to their challenge. Explore how having limited resources, while inconvenient, can actually help you move mountains with small inputs.

- *Challenge authority.* It's been said that sacred cows make the best hamburgers. What if the "grown-ups" who run everything are completely wrong? What if they're missing the big point? Often, a great starting point is to understand that the experts, the guilds, the establishment are clueless.

- *Look at the larger picture.* Zoom out. Then zoom out farther. And again. What are you actually trying to achieve? Step back a few clicks more to understand the context? Ask bigger questions. Jeff Speck, urban planner and author of *Walkable City*, suggested in a tweet[70] how we can shift our questions about transportation and city design:

Small brain: *How many cars can we move?*

Big brain: *How many people can we move?*

Galactic brain: *Why do we need to move people? Put their daily needs close at hand.*

In his inaugural address, John Kennedy challenged citizens to re-frame how they relate to their government and the nation: "... ask not what your country can do for you — ask what you can do for your country." A citizen answering the first question may want to pay less in taxes but the second question may inspire her to volunteer with the Peace Corps.

View the world differently

When is a tree a monk? The people at Interfaith Power and Light tell about their work with Buddhist monks who mobilize Cambodian communities to save their forests. For years Buddhist "eco-monks" have been working to preserve threatened forests, wildlife, and watersheds. As part of their calling, they help local people understand the value of their environment and work with them to regenerate it. One thing in particular: They ordain trees. Once ordained, the tree is seen as sacred—and protected. I feel lucky to count among my many mentors Frances Moore Lappé, democracy advocate and author, and I'm certain that hundreds of others share that feeling. As we worked on different projects over the years, I learned of the connections between our diet and world hunger, the environment, grassroots activism, and democracy. In her book *EcoMind*,[71] she also talks about how trees are seen, this time in Niger, a country that is three-fourths desert. Lappé describes how poor farmers had "regreened" 12.5 million acres:

> ...a farmer-managed strategy has revived a centuries-old practice of leaving selected tree stumps in fields and protecting their strongest stems as they grow. The renewed trees then help protect the soil, bringing big increases in crop yields, and they provide fruit, nutritious leaves, fodder, and firewood.

She asks why they hadn't figured this out long ago?

> Well, they had. But in the early twentieth century, French colonial rulers turned trees into state property and punished anyone messing with them. So farmers began to see trees as a risk to be avoided and just got rid of them. But Niger gained its independence in 1960, and over time... farmers' perceptions changed. They feel now they own the trees in their fields."

Lappé reports that the farmers have nurtured the growth of around 200 million trees. Trees once seen as risk are now seen as the path to success. "The visionary is the only realist," said Federico Fellini.

Look for the positive deviant

A number of approaches, such as positive deviance, appreciative inquiry, and asset mapping share a core idea: Instead of fixating on (then trying to fix) problems, look for what's going well and build on that. In facing a tough social challenge, positive deviance tells us to look for any outliers who may be like everyone else but who found a solution through their successful behavior. The

Positive Deviance Collaborative[72] defines these positive deviants as "individuals, groups, or entities who are the least likely to prevent or overcome a widely shared problem but are successful despite facing the same or worse challenges and barriers. They have access to the same or fewer resources than other colleagues, peers, or entities." The classic example of positive deviance involves Jerry Sternin's 1990 trip to Vietnam for Save the Children. He was given just six months to create a program that addressed inadequate diets of children in villages where 65 percent of them were malnourished. Using the positive deviance model, Sternin and his team surveyed the health of the children in the targeted villages and found some "very very poor children" who were nevertheless well nourished—positive deviants. They explored deeper with six of these families and found that their parents were gathering small shrimps, snails, or crabs in the rice paddies and adding them, along with greens, to the same meal the other children ate. These "deviant" families also fed their children three or four times a day instead of the traditional two. Yet these simple (and free) practices were available to all families. With the six-month clock ticking, the Sternin team called the village leaders and volunteers together....and did something different. "We have all learned many valuable secrets about how to have a well-nourished child despite poverty... over the past two months," he said. "But we don't know the best way to help people practice them. What should we do?" Within a couple of weeks, the village leaders had developed a roll-out plan, their way, for their community's unique challenge. By the end of the year, most of the thousand children in the program had visible improvement. The approach worked, thanks to engaging invested stakeholders in the solution and making them "the heroes."

Arvind Singhal teaches about positive deviance at the University of Texas at El Paso. He tells[73] of one of his students whose mother had died of breast cancer when she was young. The student lived in a Hispanic community where the use of cancer screening through mammograms and pap smears was low. These were the technical ways to address prevention, says Singhal, but she focused her research project from a social angle—in a zip code with low-income, little health insurance, and where few women go for cancer screenings. Her research question was: Despite the demographic and social factors that put them at risk, were there any women who had had a few cancer screenings in the past few years? "Of course, those are the deviants, the positive ones, because they're not the norm." says Singhal. What was different, deviant, about those who actually went for cancer screenings? It turned out to be their daughters. The student found that because their daughters were the ones with smartphones, and knew that they would need to take care of their mother if she fell sick, they would arrange for the test, drive mom to the clinic, and accompany her through the procedure. Once the deviants are identified, groups can then focus on building on the successful practice so others can benefit. The odd one out actually may be pointing to the solution, if we only know to look for the positive deviants.

Mapping what's really there

"Asset mapping" is a process developed in the early nineties to help a community discover its strengths and potentials. Instead of focusing on the problems, such as unemployment or crime, this participatory approach focuses on the positives, discovering the things that can help the community build on its strengths. A community asset is anything that's already present and could improve the life of a community. So what kinds of assets could you look for? Teresa Cutts has led community health asset mapping processes in Africa and around the United States and is a researcher at Wake Forest School of Medicine. She points out that asset mapping "allows us to make visible not only the tangible assets but the intangible assets." The clinic on the corner is tangible, according to Cutts, but how patients are treated is intangible. "In Africa, people would walk many kilometers to a mission hospital to receive care instead of going to a government hospital that's more convenient and better resourced but that treated them shabbily," she said. "The asset was the way the care is delivered. This form of mapping also allows us to make visible and better connect the relationships and social capital of not only providers but also those who seek care." Assets come in several forms, including:

People. The number one asset for any effort, especially on a community scale, is people. And it's all about relationships! Each person brings different gifts to the common purpose. The tribe of world change is made of many types (and, hopefully, each of us has several strengths).

Physical. A community asset can be a structure or a place like a school building, church, grocery store, or hair salon where people talk, spread ideas, and care for one another. Perhaps it's an abandoned railroad that could be turned into a hiking and biking path to create a healthier community. Almost every American city is currently rediscovering the asset of its once-abandoned urban center. In 2009, when Tony Goldman was looking for a way to revitalize a district of abandoned warehouses in Miami, he realized they had one asset in abundance: blank walls. So he invited artists to paint murals. The result? Wynwood, a giant outdoor art museum and attraction. Now, dozens of internationally-known muralists and graffiti artists have created an amazing multi-block art district.

Institutions. Organizations, schools, businesses, government agencies, and nonprofits provide critical services for a community. They run buses, shelter people experiencing homelessness, and teach our children. They also serve as networking nodes. One December afternoon in 2015, in the conference room of a small business in a Hispanic area of Winston-Salem, North Carolina nine people sat around the table. They included a couple of police officials, two hospital chaplains, the head of the Hispanic league, a local entrepreneur, and a few others. The group had been working more than a year on a plan to provide ID cards to undocumented workers in Forsyth County. The first ID sign-up drive was just weeks away and they hoped 400 people would sign up that first day. It was an awkward time politically in conservative communities for some to show the slightest support for such an initiative, so the conversation was nuanced. Not an official government ID, these cards would be issued by a nonprofit and would be recognized by the police and sheriff's office, hospitals, and other agencies. It was a small but real step forward that worked for the institutions at the time—both physical institutions and ideological ones.

These important assets—this unique assemblage of groups large and small—wouldn't have shown up in a directory or on a satellite map. They emerged and were recruited as a result of the mapping process in the neighborhood. The ID effort emerged as a priority "next step" at the end of a community health asset mapping process led by Teresa Cutts and Francis Rivers the previous summer. Card-holders would be able to get most prescriptions filled. If stopped by local law enforcement officers, they could present the ID and save everyone unnecessary problems. While the IDs couldn't be used to get a driver's license or open a bank account, they could help overcome the fear of getting crosswise with the law. The stakeholders—including leaders from the Hispanic community, hospitals and public health, the sheriffs and police departments, and others—borrowed the ID program's template from FaithAction, an organization based in Greensboro, the next city over. FaithAction lent its expertise, along with photo and computer technology and equipment, as well as a few seasoned volunteers for the first sign-up day. On a cold Friday in 2016, people holding their passports, utility bills, and other documents began forming lines at five o'clock in the morning. By five o'clock that afternoon, 580 cards had been issued. Since then, many other drives have helped several thousand more feel safer, more connected to their community, and more likely to seek necessary healthcare.

Cultural. Often overlooked, invisible cultural norms may be among the strongest assets. They might include the power of small groups, people with special roles, strong family bonds—assets that the computer-driven strategies seldom see and often ignore. In 2011, I was on the mayor's task force to revitalize Main Street. In the seventies, like most American downtowns, Little Rock watched its businesses flee to suburban malls and strip shopping centers. Main Street had been almost dead for decades. You could walk several blocks on a Saturday or Sunday and see no people, only a few parked cars, and many boarded-up windows. Our group had a lot of passion for transforming the street into a focal point of a new vital downtown, but not much else... or so we thought. Then someone came up with the idea of a food truck festival. The last event on the street had been two decades earlier in 1992, when a campaigning President Bush (the dad!) made a whistle-stop at Capitol and Main. As a cultural phenomenon, food trucks were new and really cool! A festival wouldn't cost much, we could get some local bands, find some artists to sell their work. So our small group lined up eighteen eager trucks, generated interest from the media, rounded up a few pioneering sponsors, and created a Facebook page. The October Saturday came and the weather was fantastic. Of course, we had a great location—the street is lined with oak trees and great, old (but mostly empty) buildings. The festival was slammed! More than five thousand hungry people showed up, forming long lines. Many trucks ran out of food by early afternoon (but not Hot Dog Mike, who just kept sending his sidekicks to the store for more dogs and buns!). The bands played into the evening. Even with long lines, folks had a great time and were reintroduced to a long-forgotten city treasure. A decade later, the festival had grown to eighty-five trucks and forty-five thousand people. For many reasons, each year more businesses open and residents move in, and Main Street is well on its way to living up to its name.

Asset mapping helps people identify and mobilize what they already have, and then turn these resources into building blocks for improvement. Not a bad plan if you want to change the world!

Repurposing

As a kid in the 1960s, David Burwell watched his mother co-lead a successful nine-year effort to turn a neglected train track on Cape Cod into the Shining Sea Bikeway. Federal legislation in the 1980s made it easier for railroad companies to abandon tracks and help groups convert these lines into trails for public use. This caught the attention of Burwell, Peter Harnik, and others who began attending a monthly brown-bag lunch in Washington, D.C., to explore the possibilities. In 1986, Burwell and Harnik founded Rails to Trails Conservancy (RTC) to help communities bring into reality imagined dreams of both urban and connecting trails. Since its beginnings, the number of rail-trails has grown from two hundred to more than sixteen hundred. Today with 160 thousand members, Rails to Trails has helped create a nationwide web of about 24 thousand miles of trails, and has ambitions for thousands more. Rather than discarding something after its usefulness, repurposing can open new opportunities, often in surprising ways. When these rail lines were built, who could have imagined that decades later communities would celebrate their conversion to paths for bicycles?

Repurposing is an ancient practice—animal bones became valuable tools and weapons. In a time of scarcity, scraps of cloth were sewn together into warm, colorful quilts. Used clothing converts into much hipper "vintage" garb. Old military bases were repurposed to new uses, such as Austin's airport and the Presidio in San Francisco. And buildings get green "points" for repurposing old materials in their construction. For years, Goodwill, The Arc, Habitat for Humanity's ReStore, and Big Brothers Big Sisters have repurposed our clothes, furniture, and other stuff. And they've created jobs, reduced our landfills, and raised funds for worthy causes. What can your cause creatively repurpose? What can you see that the rest of us don't?

Wow Projects

My friend Gerald did a Wow Project in his backyard. It's a long, winding garden path of stone walls, trees, fountains, and surprises—walls sculpted from rusted metal gears, spoons embedded in stone. He started the garden as a "creative expression, more than anything else," he told me, and worked on it for about twenty years. In contrast with a typical, mediocre backyard, this one makes you say, *Wow!...* over and again. In 1999, management consultant Tom Peters described the "Wow Project" in a *Fast Company* article.[74] The idea is to take on some drab assignment no one else wants and turn it into something that not only adds value, but also makes people say, *Wow!* You may have an idea you're passionate about, at work, at home, anywhere. How can you turn it into something amazing? "Project work is the vehicle by which the powerless gain power," says Peters. "Volunteer for every lousy project that comes along: Organize the office Christmas party. (Turn that dreadful holiday party into an event that says, 'Thanks for a terrific year!' to all employees.)"

Wow Projects can range from something as small as cooking an unforgettable meal, to a grand scale, such as Wangari Maathai's Green Belt movement in Kenya that planted 50 million trees. You are, according to Peters, the portfolio of your Wow Projects. Every assignment or mundane challenge—a board presentation, an e-newsletter, expanding your reading, that bare spot in the yard where nothing grows—has the potential to be a Wow Project when you decide to create something amazing and cool. The point, said Peters, "is not to do a 'good job' of managing the project that your boss dumped into your lap. It's to use every project opportunity that you can get your hands on to create surprising new ways of looking at old problems."

Again, the frameworks and ways to explore listed in this chapter are just a few. We could have just as easily looked at design thinking, appreciative inquiry, leading causes of life, liberating structures, mind maps, or many others. *Which* process you use matters less than an attitude of on-the-ground curiosity about how to make your patch of the world a better place.

CHAPTER NINE

It's all about people: community

"What must we do to evoke the greatest potential from ourselves and from others?"

—Jonas Salk

World change doesn't come about because of a single person working alone. Period. It simply doesn't happen. Individuals can pioneer new ways of thinking or doing, share their visions, act with courage and lead, but they can't make a dent in the great challenges by themselves. It's the community—yes, sometimes formed around the work of an individual—that creates lasting progress. Many artists, writers, and musicians know the energy of connecting with others who share their passion. They have found inspiration from each other in hundreds of "colonies" and communities from Paris to Taos.

One such community was the Inklings, an informal group of writers who met in the nineteen thirties and forties and included J.R.R. Tolkien and C.S. Lewis. At their tea-drinking and pipe-smoking Thursday night gatherings in Lewis' suite at Oxford University, they took turns reading manuscripts of works in progress. On any given evening they might hear a poem, a draft passage from *The Lord of the Rings*, or a portion of *The Screwtape Letters* and then offer feedback. On Tuesdays, they gathered midday in the back room of nearby pub Eagle and Child for lunch and more discussions. Over these cups of tea and pints of beer, the Inklings discussed not only their current writing, but also theories of imagination, the worlds of elves and devils, life on Mars. They struggled to understand faith, evil, and the two great wars of the twentieth century. They explored symbols and metaphors and how the power of myth and imagination frame our experience. This sharing over the years helped evoke the best work from the Inklings.

If we're lucky we are part of such a community of shared interest, one that nourishes and prods. Communities of cause vary wildly. People are attracted to a common goal: preserving or improving something, helping somebody, bringing about a slice of justice. In some, like the Catholic Worker, volunteers live together to address a range of poverty and justice issues. Some communities form around a local concern or support for the neighborhood school. Others form as people scattered far and wide gather online. The pandemic helped us to embrace community in a whole new way and at an all new level. The world became our team. We contributed to and enriched each other.

Find your community (or create it)

> "Never doubt that a small group of thoughtful, committed citizens can change the world. Indeed, it is the only thing that ever has."

This familiar quote is from Margaret Mead. She understood the power of community in part because, as an anthropologist, she observed it closely, but also because she practiced it. Mead was herself a great tribe assembler who helped create her own "small group of thoughtful, committed citizens." She told biographer Jane Howard "I make, I suppose, an average of one new friend of importance every two or three months. That's five or six good friends a year, without dropping any of the others. On the whole, I try to introduce them to each other."[75] Howard noted:

> Her generosity was staggering… She gave of her time and attention, and made connections no one else would have imagined. She picked and chose, assembled and combined and juxtaposed, with breathtaking skill. Her idea of a room was one where people looked well together, and they looked best of all if they happened to have been gathered by Margaret Mead herself.

If you're already part of a community that shares your interest, enjoy it, contribute to it, and be on the lookout for that straggler who also needs that connection. Be inviting and generous. If you're not part of a community, you may want to find one. Show up. Go to places and events where people who share your interest go. It may mean volunteering, taking a class, or going to a conference. Not only will you learn something, but you'll meet the folks involved with your cause. And then, like Margaret Mead, figure out who's worth getting to know better. If you can't find your tribe, you may have to create it. There's no magic formula and it can't be forced. At first, your group may be so loose it takes imagination to see it. Like Mead, assemble, combine, and juxtapose people. Get them into the same space and introduce them. Relationships are the bedrock of community and they don't happen overnight. They grow with trust, especially as a group takes on a project together. Mead's citizen-power is not about large numbers, it's about thoughtfulness, sharing, acting together.

People who bring life

Who do you hang out with? Do you nourish and stretch each other? Do you help each other get through challenges and move toward dreams? Pick your friends well and it can change your life. Scientists Nicholas Christakis and James Fowler in *Connected*[76] describe how social networks shape our lives. From a sample of more than three thousand people, they found that "the average American has just four close social contacts, with most having between two and six.... with whom they could discuss important matters or spend free time." About half of these were "friends" while "the other half included a wide variety of different kinds of relationships, including spouses, partners, parents, siblings, children, coworkers, fellow members of clubs, neighbors, and professional advisers and consultants." Our lives are profoundly influenced by the company we keep, as our habits and attitudes rub off on each other. Christakis and Fowler concluded that "each happy friend a person has increases that person's probability of being happy by about 9 percent. Each unhappy friend decreases it by 7 percent.... we find that having more friends is not enough—having more *happy* friends is the key to our own emotional well-being."

Who do you want to become? We can increase our chances of success by being around people we want to be like. If you want to be more positive and creative, surround yourself with positive and creative people. And being around people who smoke or do yoga increases your chances on taking up those habits. "Relationships matter because the people you spend time with shape who you are and who you become," said LinkedIn cofounder Reid Hoffman and venture capitalist Ben Casnocha in *The Start-up of You*. "Behavior and beliefs are contagious: you easily 'catch' the emotional state of your friends, imitate their actions, and absorb their values as your own. If your friends are the types of people who get stuff done, chances are you'll be that way, too. The fastest way to change yourself is to hang out with people who are already the way you want to be."[77]

If you happen to be in a role of hiring staff, recruiting key volunteers, or contracting outside vendors, consider that every position you have is a precious gift. A cause's most valuable asset is its collection of people, so a leader's first job is finding and keeping the most insanely-talented folks possible. Most nonprofits are on tight budgets and staff is often the largest expense, so it's doubly important. While experience, degrees, and résumés matter, focus on talent, attitude, and energy. All of us fall somewhere along an energy spectrum. Avoid those on the *decelerator* end who will drag your effort down. Only bring on *accelerators* who can push your cause forward. Build a diverse team with weird people and misfits. The caption under Sigourney Weaver's high school yearbook portrait[78] said: *Please, God, please, don't let me be normal.* Find passionate people already doing amazing things on their own (it's a sign of life). Did he perform in an opera? Does she go hang gliding on the weekends? Look for people who are smarter than you, happy and awake. Gather those who believe in your mission and will add energy to your efforts. The leader's second job is to guarantee a culture that helps those talented people thrive as they engage the mission. That includes making sure they have the tools they need. It's been said, a good leader also provides air cover for the team to protect them from the assaults of bureaucracy and time-wasting activities, and to free them to do their important work.

Cynics chill, but activists persist

We all know someone who repeatedly tries—and sometimes succeeds—to make us feel bad about our efforts and ideals. We may have felt their small comment crush our spirit. Ray Bradbury tells us to ditch those bad "friends." Speaking to an audience of aspiring writers he offered this advice: "Get rid of those friends of yours who make fun of you and don't believe in you. When you leave here tonight, go home, make a phone call and fire them. Anyone who doesn't believe in you and your future, to hell with them!" Follow this advice and you will look back in a few months with a sigh of relief, having cut loose a source of dragging negativity.

But another source of cynicism is closer to home. And it may be fueled by the messages we get from the airwaves. In a "Fresh Air" interview,[79] singer/songwriter and activist Billy Bragg said that our biggest enemy is our own cynicism, "…our own sense that nothing will ever change, that nobody cares about this stuff, that all politicians are the same." Bragg said that right wing media want you to believe that "nobody else cares. That's why they have a… low-level war on empathy. If anyone talks about anything compassionate, they dismiss it as political correctness or virtue signaling…. They want us to feel cynical about the world and that nothing can be done." To make a difference, he offered, "We have to be able to overcome that…and go out every day and think the glass is half full." Hope, trust, and determination are the antidote to cynicism. While our knowledge may not be complete, we can still act on what we do know—even when we don't have a spreadsheet to prove it to a cynic.

Negative people may be cynics, pessimists, back-stabbers, scape-goaters, know-it-alls, liars, get-ahead-at-other's-expensers, or just mean people. And having these folks on your team can go beyond just being unpleasant and slowing things down: It can derail an entire effort. Unable to see people's goodness and sincerity, cynics believe people aren't trustworthy and are motivated only by self-interest. Cynicism leads to inaction, often hiding behind "being realistic." And pessimists see only the worst in all situations and potential outcomes. They know nothing good can ever happen, that only a quixotic fool would try to make a difference in the world. To be fair, none of us is free of these negative traits;

we all struggle. Our cynicism or pessimism comes from our wound-edness and we must tend these wounds. But we can choose our friends and, to a degree, we can choose our colleagues and our partners in social change. If we're serious about fixing the world, we should be deliberate about who's on the team. Bill Foege said, "There is a place for cynicism and pessimism. But whenever you need it, contract for it. Don't get those people on your payroll."[80]

When President Lincoln issued the Emancipation Proclamation, he was in part showing courage and in part playing a role that events had thrust upon him, built on a century of abolitionists' unceasing work. But when, with the stroke of the pen, millions of slaves were freed, even many anti-slavery advocates were surprised. Abolitionist Ralph Waldo Emerson called it something "most of us dared not hope to see." There is a great gap between a cynic, who in Emerson's words "can chill and dishearten with a single word," and a believer who, like Emerson, doesn't dare to get his hopes too high, yet still toils year after year to accomplish the goal.

Cascading connections

From time to time, opportunities just show up at the door of any group that's plugging away, doing good work. Someone shows up with a unique set of skills, an unexpected major gift, or an invitation to partner with another organization. And sometimes people want to introduce you to their friends. I once explored a winding road of such sharing. In the fall of 2008 at Heifer International, we'd noticed some gifts—a few thousand dollars—coming in from the blog of *New York Times* bestselling fantasy author Patrick Rothfuss. I called to thank him and quickly learned he was a consummate people person and was recruiting fellow fantasy and sci-fi authors to donate signed books and other literary objects of desire. These were being auctioned off to fans with the proceeds going to Heifer. Rothfuss had pledged $5,000 to match what they gave. "It just snowballed," Rothfuss recently told Jason Woods of Heifer International.[81] By the end of that first year people had given more than $50,000. "I matched all of it, and it used up all my money. It was a good feeling. It was a real good feeling." Rothfuss told Woods that he "was unaware at the time that taxes are not taken out of book royalties. 'That was a very near miss, I almost went to jail for not paying taxes and stuff,' he said. 'But I've done dumber things for not nearly as good reasons.'" He and a few volunteers tracked the activity and shipped the books from his home to readers around the country. In that first call, I asked Rothfuss where he heard about Heifer. He said had seen a music video by singer Sarah McLachlan that included a few mentions of Heifer. We knew of the video. And before that, McLachlan had done a photo shoot for us, and her aunt had served on Heifer's board of directors. Rothfuss had shown this video in his university class and later, when he mentioned it to his mom, he learned that she'd been a long-time supporter through her church.

Meanwhile, and unrelated, fantasy author Neil Gaiman had heard about Heifer from two different sources—a blog he'd read and an honor gift card from a friend—and had posted a bit about Heifer on his own blog. So in a second call with Rothfuss, I told him that Neil Gaiman was also a Heifer fan. Rothfuss told me he'd recently met Gaiman, so he reached out and told him of the fundraiser. Gaiman then posted about the campaign and soon many of his fans got involved. (Amongst them was Zoe Elkaim, who was online publicist for her mother, the popular mystery writer Laurie King. Elkaim reached out to Heifer to start a different campaign to coincide with Sir Arthur Conan Doyle's 150th birthday. This raised another $30,000 over the next two years.) Others got involved in the Rothfuss campaign: The *Wheel of Time* book series ran an auction; the band Creed donated a signed guitar; and pretty much every sci-fi or fantasy writer (including George R.R. Martin) seemed to have joined the effort. So by the end of the first two years, the combined efforts had raised more than $300,000 to help struggling families around the world. Ten years later, Rothfuss's efforts have raised $10 million and Heifer is a favored cause among fantasy, sci-fi, and comics fans. While this example includes celebrities and big numbers, this kind of cascading connections happens at every scale to causes that are regarded as important. If you think you see one, take some time to explore it. Like me, you'll probably find some surprises in your community.

Ask for help

Communities work because we help each other. Too often seen as a weakness, asking for help—and being willing to help when asked—is necessary to do great things. In the acknowledgements section of her best-selling book *Quiet*,[82] Susan Cain thanks more than two hundred people by name. Along the way, she had asked them to help her share contacts, read some pages, be a sounding board, do an interview. A self-described introvert, Cain reached out to friends and strangers to accomplish her goal. Why is asking so hard? Over the years, I have watched a friend help hundreds of people. No one is more giving. Yet... "Asking for help is one of the things I find very difficult," she told me. "There have been times when I felt totally wiped out, discouraged, depressed, or overwhelmed. Usually, instead of asking for help, I end up having a good cry and making some kind of new plan to deal with issues myself. It is easier to give help than to ask for it." It *is* uncomfortable. Deep in the American psyche are the pioneers surviving heroically in isolation on the open prairie. In a culture that reveres self-reliance, seeking help is admitting that we depend on others. We're afraid we'll be seen as weak, unable, or incompetent. There are so many reasons we don't ask.

Does it make it any easier when you're asking for a cause? "For me this is not just a book; it's a mission," Susan Cain told journalist Jeff Glor for CBS News:

> I was fueled by the same mix of passion and indignation that I imagine inspired Betty Friedan to publish *The Feminine Mystique* in 1963. Introverts are to extroverts what women were to men at that time—second-class citizens with gigantic amounts of untapped talent. Our schools, workplaces, and religious institutions are designed for extroverts, and many introverts believe that there is something wrong with them and that they should try to "pass" as extroverts. The bias against introversion leads to a colossal waste of talent, energy, and happiness.[83]

Many of those who helped Cain resonated with her cause: to improve life for the half of our population who are introverts. But first, she had to explain her mission, her book—and ask each one for help! We're much more likely to accomplish something significant when we get beyond ourselves. This is especially true when it comes to growing support for our cause. In asking for help, we invite others to be part of something important.

Through the explosion of crowdfunding, nonprofits and others have created new ways to ask for help. An alternative to traditional financing, crowdfunding allows you to raise money for a new venture or project from many people in a short time. And some crowd support takes the form of volunteering. To see how far volunteer supporters can take a cause, look at the world of knowledge. *The Encyclopedia Britannica* was first published around 1770. Not long ago it had a staff of about a hundred editors along with four thousand paid contributors. But it recently quit its print operation. Why? Largely because crowd-sourced Wikipedia has exponentially more information: At the time of this writing, it's equal to 2,955 volumes of EB and is rapidly growing. It's more up to date and, with real-time peer review, is just as accurate. A *Wiki* (the Hawaiian word for fast) is a collaborative software, like the one Wikipedia, founded in 2001 by Larry Sanger and Jimmy Wales, is built on. The founders' goal was to provide a free encyclopedia to every person on the planet because, well, knowledge is power. A nonprofit with a staff of 450, Wikipedia is the fifth largest website in the world, with millions of articles in dozens of languages. How is this possible? Wikipedia asks for and depends on roughly 120 thousand active volunteers to contribute content and editing. Of course, the Wiki community didn't stop there. Wikibooks is focused on creating free textbooks, Wikimedia Commons is a repository for free images and other media, Wiktionary is a dictionary and thesaurus, Wikiversity is a collection of learning tools, Wikispecies is a dictionary of forms of life, just to name a few. This sharing of time and information has transformed our access to knowledge—all because people ask for help.

Wicked problems

"When one tugs at a single thing in nature, he finds it attached to the rest of the world."

—John Muir

A former teacher, Lily Eskelsen García, was president of the National Education Association. Representing public school teachers, the NEA is the country's largest labor union. At a Campaign for America's Future event, she told about the time she found herself sitting next to a talkative businessman on a plane.[84]

He's telling me where he's going and what he's doing and what his business is. And he says, "So what do you do, Darlin'?"

I said, "Well, I'm a teacher. And now I work with the National Education Association.

145

He stopped smiling and he said, "I've heard about you people."
He said, "I hear you need this and I hear you need that. Then
I hear you need something else. To tell you the truth, Darlin',
I'm getting tired of hearing it. I'm a businessman. I want you
to bottom line it for me. I want you to tell me right now what
is the one single thing that would solve all of our problems in
public schools?"

I said, "That's easy, what we really need are fewer people who
think there's one single thing that would solve all of our problems in public schools."

In 1973, UC Berkeley professors, Horst Rittel and Melvin
Webber, published a paper describing *Wicked Problems*.[85] They said
that the traditional scientific approach doesn't work in solving
social problems. Problem-solving in the industrial age focused on
efficiency, and the challenges our scientists and engineers address
are similar. They all focus on "tame" or "benign" problems, such
as solving a mathematical equation or analyzing the chemical
structure of an organic compound. For these, they say, "the mission
is clear. It's clear, in turn, whether or not the problems have been
solved." On the other hand, a wicked problem is one that's not
easy to describe, it has many causes, it's hard or impossible to
"solve." It occurs in a social context where diverse stakeholders
understand it differently.

For example, explore what's facing your local public schools and
you may quickly find yourself tangled in a web of issues: lack of support, privatization, White flight, teachers unions, and vaccine and
mask mandates. Public schools find themselves underfunded,
undercut, under attack. And, of course, there's poverty. Poverty
adds daily challenges to students and their families. It thwarts whole
communities, complicating everything. Add to these voting rights,
political influence, who controls the school board and the media,
and grassroots organizing. This simple description here reflects my
own biases. You likely see public schools from a different angle.

Another person, say, the businessman on the plane, sees it differently from you and me. We all view the challenge in our unique way, and this adds to the wickedness of the challenges facing public schools. Pull on a single thread of any wicked problem and you quickly discover you're pulling many, many threads. "Imagine a multidimensional spider's web in the early morning covered with dew drops," said Alan Watts. "And every dew drop contains the reflection of all the other dew drops. And, in each reflected dew drop, the reflections of all the other dew drops in that reflection. And so ad infinitum. That is the Buddhist conception of the universe in an image." It's also what a wicked problem can look like. Each piece reflects and connects to the others. And when you find yourself in one of these complex tangles, deciding what action to take can be overwhelming. "Doing the right thing is not the problem," said President Lyndon Johnson. "Knowing what the right thing is, that's the challenge." Here are some of the characteristics of wicked problems Horst Rittel and Melvin Webber presented:

- There is no definitive formulation of a wicked problem.

- Solutions to wicked problems are not true or false, but good or bad [or better or worse].

- Every solution to a wicked problem is a "one-shot operation"; because there is no opportunity to learn by trial-and-error, every attempt counts significantly.

- Every wicked problem is essentially unique.

- Every wicked problem can be considered to be a symptom of another problem.

Stability and justice in the Middle East, affordable quality health care in the United States, economic disparity, racism, women's rights, homelessness—wicked problems, every one. As is any fractal piece of any of these. Mahatma Gandhi didn't "solve" his challenges of both independence and convincing Indians to live in harmony. Martin Luther King didn't solve his challenges. Neither have Gloria Steinem, Mother Teresa, Caesar Chavez, Al Gore, or Malala Yousafzai. But, along with their communities, they all took on wicked problems, and we live in a better world because of their work.

Parts of a grand Movement

As wickedly connected as our challenges are, the movement's connections can be stronger as people of every kind gather in a vast commons to work for more justice, peace, and sustainability. In *Blessed Unrest*, environmental and social justice leader Paul Hawken speaks of this larger movement as "a coalescence comprising hundreds of thousands of organizations" that "claims no special powers and arises in small discrete ways, like blades of grass after a rain." The movement is a collective consciousness and action for good.

> The movement grows and spreads in every city and country, and involves virtually every tribe, culture, language, and religion, from Mongolians to Uzbeks to Tamils. It is composed of families in India, students in Australia, farmers in France, the landless in Brazil, the Bananeras of Honduras, the "poors" of Durban, villagers in Irian Jaya, indigenous tribes of Bolivia, and housewives in Japan. Its leaders are farmers, zoologists, shoemakers, and poets. It provides support and meaning to billions of people in the world.
>
> The movement can't be divided because it is so atomized—a collection of small pieces, loosely joined. It forms, dissipates and then regathers quickly, without central leadership, command or control. Rather than seeking dominance, this unnamed movement strives to disperse concentrations of power. It has been capable of bringing down governments, companies, and leaders through witnessing, informing, and massing. The quickening of the move-

ment in recent years has come about through information technologies becoming increasingly accessible and affordable to people everywhere. Its clout resides in its ideas, not in force.[86]

Because all movements converge into one Movement, progress in one can boost progress in another. With its millions of parts, this vast movement struggles daily against injustice, racism, greed, poisoning the planet, violations of dignity. Whether you are teaching disabled children or undergirding people's right to vote, you are linked to one hyper-complex system. This "blessed unrest," or as civil rights activist and congressman John Lewis called it "good trouble," is the mirror image of wicked problems. The big flip is to be as smart about being blessed as the wicked problems are about being evil.

As parts of the vast Movement, all movements connect. Like Russian dolls, each movement nests in larger movements and serves as a nest for smaller ones. The nested aspect of movements is about their family, their rootedness, like a tree. The better nutrition from the roots and leaves from the related movements, the healthier that particular movement is. In turn, it boosts those in its nesting tree. People drawn to one are also drawn to its branches and off-shoots. So, the microbrewery in your town is nested in the larger local beer movement, that's nested in the local food movement, which is nested in the buy local movement, and so on.

All movements also brush into others horizontally, creating blurred edges. The CDC tells us that over the last three decades childhood obesity has doubled among children and quadrupled among adolescents. The one-third of American children and adolescents who are overweight or obese are more vulnerable to health challenges like diabetes, and other consequences. Many movements connect to this: the movement to get kids more physically active; the last-child-in-the-woods/save-children-from-nature-deficit-disorder movement, the quit-advertising-junk-food-to-kids movement, the healthy food movement, the schoolyard garden movement, and so on. We could have listed an additional thirty sub-movements and stayed right next to the childhood obesity efforts. Each movement has its own experts, research, books, websites, organizations, conferences, goals, cultures, and most important, passionate people. But these movements are far from isolated. The energy from one spills over to help related movements, especially when they work together. A community health group asking the city council to invest more in walking paths is joined by another group describing the positive impact walkable neighborhoods have on economic development. Each movement has friends and, sometimes, foes. Movements already share many of the same supporters. How do you *together* accomplish more?

Find a good partner for any worthwhile cause and you'll soon learn that two are stronger than one. Partners bring new assets to the effort, creating greater possibility. The chemical reaction from the different agents often creates something new, more powerful. Of course, not all partners make sense. You may be in an organization that holds endless debates: Would we partner with this or that corporation, the government, a competitor? Abolitionist and writer Frederick Douglas said, "I will unite with anyone to do good, but with no one to do harm." You'll have to find your right place on this (perhaps by trial and error). Be creative and open minded about potential partners. In *Beautiful Trouble*,[87] organizer for social justice and ecology movements Joshua Kahn Russell suggests that we think of groupings. "Successful movement-building hinges on being able to see a society in terms of specific blocs or networks, some of which are institutions (unions, churches, schools), others of which are less visible or cohesive, like youth subcultures or demographic groupings."

On the surface, a retirement center and an elementary school may seem an unlikely pair for improving the world, but in *The Element*,[88] leader in education and creativity Ken Robinson and author Lou Aronica tell of a retirement center owner in Jenks,

Oklahoma who offered to help kids in the school across the street. With the school district's consent, they set up a glass-walled classroom for preschoolers and kindergartners in the lobby of the retirement center. The program paired an elderly resident with a child for one-on-one activities, including reading in turn. The results are inspiring: The elders now find something to look forward to when they get up in the morning and are taking fewer medications. And the kids? "More than 70 percent are leaving the program at age five reading at a third-grade level or higher," said Robinson and Aronica. "But the children are learning much more than how to read. As they sit with their book buddies, the kids have rich conversations with the adults." Every once in a while, the authors report, the children are also told that one of their buddies has passed. The program "has restored an ancient, traditional relationship between the generations. The very young and the very old have always had an almost mystical connection." Both the retirement center and the school had untapped community assets— elderly residents and young children—that, when aligned, achieved powerful outcomes for each institution and for the broader community.

Elderly residents are also helping younger people who want to learn English. The Brazilian language organization CNA Speaking Exchange connects their students through video chat with seniors who live in retirement centers in the United States. The students get direct practice and the seniors get someone to talk with, some forming relationships that have lasted for years. And in Deventer, Netherlands, six college students live rent-free in a retirement home alongside 160 residents. The students "spend at least thirty hours each month helping their fellow residents," Anne-Marie Botek wrote in AgingCare.[89] "Their assignment is to 'be a good neighbor,'" said [director Gea] Sijkpes, who now gets letters and messages from hundreds of students who also want to live at Humanitas... Sijkpes said the program has helped create 'the warmest and nicest nursing home of Deventer.'" Botek reported that one student "developed such a deep connection with one of the older women in the community that she asked the woman to be the flower girl in her wedding."

In exploring partnerships, ask what do you have to offer? What are you looking for in an ally? Once you've identified a potential partner, do your due diligence, especially making sure you are in sync in terms of values and ethics. Be clear about your goals, who is going to do what, boundaries, and an exit strategy. The right partners can help move a cause far beyond where it could have otherwise gone.

CHAPTER TEN

Ogres and fireflies

Years ago, waiting with my younger son in the elementary school auditorium for the holiday program to begin, I asked what he learned in school that day. "VCCV," he said. "VCCV? What's that?" You know, Vowel, Consonant, Consonant, Vowel. He looks at a banner on the auditorium wall that reads PROGRESS! "Like O-G-R-E," he said. I laughed. I had never noticed the "ogre" in "progress." But there it was right in the middle, as big as, well, an ogre! In folktales, ogres are usually large, hairy, hominid giants that are dangerous and feed on humans. The ogre is a universal creature: Native American lore includes people-eating giants, for Odysseus it was Cyclops, and in Japan it's the *oni*. It's also a metaphor for that dreaded monster that lurks in our world and has to be subdued if we want to move forward. Because ogres stand guard against progress, every social movement has to take them on. Most are subtle, almost invisible, and today they have sophisticated, well-oiled propaganda machines. Sometimes they have surveillance, prisons, and weapons.

On another level, the ogre is inside us, part of our shadow. It wants to block us from changing a habit or taking on an important challenge. When the ogre tries to eat the children, it's trying to kill our agency, our possibility. It stands between us and our own powerful growth. In *The Hero with a Thousand Faces*, mythologist Joseph Campbell says that in these stories from around the world, ogres are the "threshold guardian." The threshold stands for the "limits of hero's present sphere, of life horizon. Beyond them are darkness, the unknown, and danger."

> One had better not challenge the watcher of the established bounds. And yet—it is only by advancing beyond those bounds, provoking the other, destructive aspect of the same power, that the individual passes, either alive or in death, into a new zone of experience…. The adventure is always and everywhere a passage beyond the veil of the known into the unknown; the powers that watch at the boundary are dangerous; to deal with them is risky; yet for anyone with competence and courage the danger fades.[90]

Each of today's challenges comes with its own ogres. For example, the Ogre of Disenfranchisement wants some people to lose their vote, not count, disappear, have less power over their lives. At one point or another, group after group has battled this particular ogre in every corner of the land: Native Americans, Blacks, women, people who didn't own land, eighteen- to-twenty-one-year-olds who were being drafted to fight a war, non-Protestants, poor people, those in jail, felons who have served their sentences, and residents of Puerto Rico or Washington, D.C. Some of these struggles are yet to be resolved, but one by one, most ogres that kept Americans from voting have been defeated. To fight them, people planned, made alliances, appealed, marched, were jailed, and beaten. Many died. Women fought for decades to win suffrage. So did Blacks, and in 1965, voting rights legislation brought down giant barriers.

But, like monsters at the end of a bad movie the ogres are back. Actually, they never left. Over the last decade, disingenuous legislators across the country have scrambled to create new and improved voting barriers. This is coordinated and pretends to be guarding against massive voter fraud, a problem that doesn't even exist. The goal is to distort elections to favor the wealthy and powerful, signaling nothing less than the struggle between democracy and despotism. "The community today is the planet, not the bounded nation," said Joseph Campbell.[91] "The national idea, with the flag as totem, is today an aggrandizer of the nursery ego…. And the numerous saints of this anticult—namely the patriots whose ubiquitous photographs, draped with flags, serve as official icons—are precisely the local threshold guardians… whom it is the first problem of the hero to surpass." Authoritarianism is a danger to humankind. It's an ogre. Injustice and inequality spawn *entire colonies* of ogres. So do racism, sexism, classism, and any other *ism* that exploits people or that lessens anyone's dignity. So do the ogres that put profit before humanity and our home, Earth. These ogres guard every single threshold between where we are today, and the thriving and just world we yearn to live in.

The vast commons

This is all heavy stuff. It lies at the intersection of our current world and hope. Given everything we know, should we have hope? Are we able to hope? Imagine a giant commons, a vast place where the Movement gathers. No *one* owns it—we *all* do. There, we reflect on our impossible "heroes journeys" to bring more wholeness. We dream and share and make our bold plans for our squares in the quilt, in their infinite expressions. There, we look for help and join the causes of others. Good people doing good work alongside other good people. We find meaning and beauty and are enriched. Of course, on this vast commons you'll find mostly native species. The ogres that once lived there—English ivy, privet, kudzu, and others too alarming to name—have been defeated, sent back to where they belong. Now, we see local grasses, forbs, and stately trees. And best of all, as dusk begins to fall on a long summer evening, here come the fireflies. More than had been there for a long time. We watch them as we sit and reflect on the day's work.

On that note, you know what's cool? Homegrown National Park's choice for a logo—of course, it's the firefly! First, it's unique, singular, identifiable—all that marketing stuff. But there's more. On the one hand, many firefly species face extinction, so it's a stark reminder of the biodiversity crisis and the need for action. But it's also such a bright and hopeful symbol. And maybe in your neighborhood you'll start seeing firefly yard signs amid landscapes of oaks and wildflowers. As we boot the invasives from our yards and help the native plants come back home, we'll be living in greater harmony. Maybe not with our neighbors, at first. But certainly with nature and ourselves and what it means to flourish. And most of the neighbors will come along over time. While this particular firefly is just a symbol, it has a special feature: If we do what Homegrown National Park asks us to, in many of our yards this symbol will actually appear in person! Or in fireflyness (or whatever that would be called!). We'll see more fireflies lighting up our summer evenings—blinking signs of success—bringing a sense of magic and reminding us that, acting together, we can change the world!

Endnotes

1 Derek Sivers. "How to start a movement." TED Talk. February, 2010.

2 UN Press Release, August 9, 2021. "Secretary-General Calls Latest IPCC Climate Report 'Code Red for Humanity', Stressing 'Irrefutable' Evidence of Human Influence."

3 Vijay Prashad, Obama in India. *CounterPunch*, November 5, 2010.

4 Charles Duhigg, *The Power of Habit*. (New York: Random House, 2012) 272-3.

5 Kate Messner. "How to Build a Fictional World," TED Ed. 2014.

6 Louis Fischer. *The Life of Mahatma Gandhi*. (New York: Harper & Row, 1983) 325.

7 Jim Collins and Jerry Porras, *Built to Last* (New York: HarperCollins, 1994) 111-4.

8 Jim Collins, *Good to Great*. (New York: HarperCollins, 2001) 202.

9 Tom Peterson. 1989. "UNICEF's James Grant," *Seeds*, January/February 1989. 18-21.

10 Video interview of Bill Foege, posted by the Rockefeller Center Bellagio Center. June 23, 2014. https://www.youtube.com/watch?v= 657HJmP4gV4

11 1981 "Call to Halt the Nuclear Arms Race." Flyer and petition. https://livingwiththebomb.files.wordpress.com/2013/08/call-to-halt-arms-race.pdf

12 NASA. "NASA Langley Research Center's Contributions to the Apollo Program." https://www.nasa.gov/centers/langley/news/fact-sheets/Apollo.html

13 CNN. April, 17, 2019. "The most effective way to tackle climate change? Plant 1 trillion trees." Mark Tutton.

14 "The Cosmic Calendar." *Wikipedia.* https://en.wikipedia.org/wiki/Cosmic_Calendar

15 UN Media Release. "Nature's Dangerous Decline 'Unprecedented'; Species Extinction Rates 'Accelerating'" May 6, 2019. Intergovernmental Science-Policy Platform on Biodiversity and Ecosystem Services (IPBES).

16 Edward O.Wilson, *Half Earth: Our Planet's Fight for Life* (New York: Liveright Publishing, 2016). 187.

17 John D. Morse, ed. *Ben Shahn* (New York: Praeger Publishers, 1972) 92.

18 Amar Prabhu. 2012. "How Much Money Did Jonas Salk Potentially Forfeit By Not Patenting The Polio Vaccine?" *Forbes,* August 9, 2012.

19 Jane Howard, *Margaret Mead, A Life* (New York, Simon and Schuster, 1984) 231.

20 Scott Belsky, *Making Ideas Happen: Overcoming Obstacles Between Vision & Reality* (London: Penguin Books, 2010) 121.

21 Allison H. Fine, *Momentum: Igniting Social Change in the Connected Age* (San Francisco: Jossey-Bass, 2006) 19.

22 "Social Determinants of Health Series: Transportation and the Role of Hospitals" American Hospital Association, 2017. https://www.aha.org/ahahret-guides/2017-11-15-social-determinants-health-series-transportation-and-role-hospitals

23 Sam Tsemberis. 2012. "Housing First: Ending Homelessness, Transforming Lives, and Changing Communities" TEDx Moses Brown School.

24 Terrence McCoy, "Meet the outsider who accidentally solved chronic homelessness." *Washington Post*, May 6, 2015.

25 Abigail Tucker. 2012. "Inside the Plan to Get 100,000 Homeless Off the Streets" *Smithsonian Magazine*, June 2012.

26 Hugh MacLeod, Ignore Everybody: and 39 Other Keys to Creativity, (New York: Penguin Group, 2009).

27 Nico van Oudenhoven and Rekha Wazir. 1998. "Replicating Social Programmes: Approaches, Strategies and Conceptual Issues. Management of Social Transformations." UNESCO.

28 Candy Chang. "The Story: Artist Candy Chang shares the story of how the Before I Die project came to be." *Before I Die* website. https://beforeidieproject.com/story

29 Candy Chang. 2012. "Before I die I want to…" *TEDGlobal*, July, 2012.

30 "The Arbor Day Foundation Launches the Time for Trees Initiative to Plant 100 Million Trees by 2022" Arbor Day Foundation media release, https://www.arborday.org/media/pressreleases/press-release.cfm?id=452

31 Seth Godin. 2010. "The Truth about Shipping." 99U. https://99u.adobe.com/articles/6249/seth-godin-the-truth-about-shipping

32 Reid Hoffman and Ben Casnocha, *The Start-up of You* (New York: Crown Business, 2012) 21-2.

33 Barry Miles, *Paul McCartney: Many Years from Now* (New York: Henry Holt and Company, 1997) 171.

34 Anne Lamott, *Bird by Bird* (New York: Anchor Books, 1994) 28.

35 Used with permission of authors, Bre Pettis and Kio Stark. https://medium.com/@bre/the-cult-of-done-manifesto-724ca1c2ff13.

36 Jim Collins, *Good to Great*. (New York: HarperCollins, 2001) 164-5.

37 Jim Collins, *Good to Great*. (New York: HarperCollins, 2001) 165.

38 Daniel Goleman, *Focus: The Hidden Driver of Excellence* (New York: HarperCollins, 2013) 218-9.

39 Mary Pipher, *Writing to Change the World* (New York: Riverhead Books, 2006) 12.

40 Philip Kotler and Nancy R. Lee, *Social Marketing: Influencing Behaviors for Good* (Thousand Oaks, California, Sage Publications, 2008) 4-7.

41 Philip Kotler and Nancy R. Lee, *Social Marketing: Influencing Behaviors for Good* (Thousand Oaks, California, Sage Publications, 2008) 5.

42 Sean Rossman. "Girl Scout Cookie sales start today." *USA Today*, January 3, 2018.

43 Dan Heath and Chip Heath. "Turning Vitamins into Aspirin: Consumers and the 'Felt Need.'" *Fast Company*, November 2, 2010.

44 William Foster and Gail Fine. "How Nonprofits Get Really Big." *Stanford Social Innovation Review*, Spring 2007.

45 Nancy Duarte, *Resonate: Present Visual Stories that Transform Agencies* (Hoboken, New Jersey: John Wiley & Sons, 2010) 18-22.

46 Mary Pipher, *Writing to Change the World* (New York: Riverhead Books, 2006) 143-4.

47 Roy Williams, Secret Formulas of the Wizard of Ads. (Austin: Wizard Academy Press, 2010) 152-3.

48 Chip Heath and Dan Heath, *Made to Stick: Why some ideas survive and others die* (New York: Random House, 2007) 146-7.

49 Video interview. "Cleve Jones on Harvey Milk & AIDS Memorial Quilt." *Xtra Magazine!* 2009.

50 Garry Wills, *Certain Trumpets: The Nature of Leadership* (New York: Simon & Schuster, 1994) 13.

51 Nicholas Kristof. "Triumph of a Dreamer." *New York Times*, November 14, 2009.

52 Douglas Gayeton, *Local: The New Face of Food and Farming in America* (New York: Harper Design, 2014) 18.

53 Glenn Rifkin. "How to "Truck" the Brand: Lessons from the Grateful Dead" *Strategy + Business*, January 1, 1997.

54 "MD Anderson Cancer Center "Brand Journey" AMA Houston Lunch June 2011. https://www.slideshare.net/amahouston/md-anderson-cancer-center-brand-journey-ama-houston-lunch-june-2011

55 T.S. Eliot, *Old Possum's Book of Practical Cats* (New York: Harcourt Brace Jovanovich, 1939) 1.

56 Stephen King, *On Writing* (New York: Simon & Schuster, 2000) 110.

57 "Whose Heritage?" Southern Poverty Law Center. https://www.splcenter.org/data-projects/whose-heritage

58 Jeff Guo. "We counted literally every road in America. Here's what we learned." *Washington Post*, March 6, 2015

59 Eugene Robinson comments on NBC's "Meet the Press" June 21, 2015.

60 https://www.businessinsider.com/robert-e-lee-opposed-confederate-monuments-2017-8

61 Tony Santaella and Doug Stanglin. "Pair released on bond after removing Confederate flag at S.C. Capitol." *USA TODAY*, June 27, 2015.

62 Women on 20s Website. https://www.womenon20s.org/home

63 https://www.newsobserver.com/news/local/education/article 22503351.html

64 "Madrid begins renaming streets that honour Franco regime." *The Local [Spain]*, April 2018.

65 "Where The Streets Have Men's Names (And How To Change That)" NPR's Weekend Edition interview with Santi Van Den Toorn, August 11, 2018.

66 Howard Gardner, *Five Minds for the Future* (Boston: Harvard Business Press, 2008) 83.

67 Mihaly Csikszentmihalyi, *Creativity: Flow and the Psychology of Discovery and Invention* (New York: HarperCollins, 1996) 94.

68 Thomas Wedell-Wedellsborg. "Are You Solving the Right Problems?" *Harvard Business Review*, January-February 2017.

69 Tina Seelig. "How Reframing a Problem Unlocks Innovation." *Fast Company*, April 19, 2013.

70 Andrew Price. "We Need Complete Neighborhoods." Strong Towns, February 7, 2018.

71 Frances Moore Lappé, *EcoMind* (New York: Nation Books, 2011) 71-2.

72 Positive Deviance Collaborative. https://positivedeviance.org

73 Stakeholder Health podcast with Arvind Singhal, February 28, 2019. https://stakeholderhealth.org/arvind-singhal-positive-deviance/

74 Tom Peters. "The Wow Project." *Fast Company*, April 30, 1999.

75 Jane Howard, *Margaret Mead, A Life* (New York, Simon and Schuster, 1984) 13.

76 Nicholas Christakis and James Fowler, *Connected: The Surprising Power of Our Social Networks and How They Shape Our Lives.* (New York: Little, Brown and Company, 2009) 52.

77 Reid Hoffman and Ben Casnocha, *The Start-up of You* (New York: Crown Business, 2012) 85.

78 Lauren Zupkus, *Huffpost.* "Sigourney Weaver's High School Yearbook Quote Is All Too Fitting Now" June 20, 2014. https://www.huffingtonpost.com/2014/06/20/sigourney-weaver-yearbook-photo_n_5514914.html

79 Terry Gross interview with Billy Bragg on NPR's *Fresh Air.* June 19, 2017.

80 Bill Foege comments at 2004 Hilton Humanitarian Prize ceremony.

81 Jason Woods, "Author Pat Rothfuss on Fundraising for Heifer International via Worldbuilders" https://www.heifer.org/blog/culture/author-pat-rothfuss-on-fundraising-for-heifer-international-via-world-builders.html

82 Susan Cain, *Quiet* (New York: Crown Publishers, 2012) 273-6.

83 Jeff Glor speaks with Susan Cain about "Quiet: The Power of Introverts in a World That Can't Stop Talking." *CBS News,* January 26, 2012.

84 "NEA's Lily Eskelsen García on What Teachers Do" Video from *Campaign for America's Future*, November 3, 2015.

85 Horst W.J. Rittel & Melvin M. Webber. "Dilemmas in a general theory of planning." *Policy Sci 4*, 155–169 (1973).

86 Paul Hawken, *Blessed Unrest*, (New York: Viking Penguin, 2007) 11-2.

87 Andrew Boyd, assembler. *Beautiful Trouble: A Toolbox for Revolution* (New York: OR Books, 2012) 172-3.

88 Ken Robinson with Lou Aronica, *The Element* (New York: Penguin Books

89 Anne-Marie Botek, "Why These College Students Love Living in a Retirement Home. *AgingCare*. https://www.agingcare.com/articles/college-students-living-in-nursing-home-179924.htm

90 Joseph Campbell, *The Hero with a Thousand Faces* (Princeton: Princeton University Press, 1949) 77ff.

91 Joseph Campbell, *The Hero with a Thousand Faces* (Princeton: Princeton University Press, 1949) 388-9.

Acknowledgements

Collectively, we have brought into the world just what it needed: yet another book! But here it is. And a lot of people helped along the way, including Dora Barilla, Teresa Cutts, Gary Gunderson, Maureen Kersmarki, Mike Matchett, Peggy Scherer. A special thanks to Melanie Raskin, a great editor, and to HK Stewart for design-through-production and more. And thanks to my students at the Clinton School of Public Service for your passion and intelligence. And thanks to of the many incredible colleagues I've had along the way for caring about our world and sharing your lives.

About the Author

Anonprofit leader and strategist, **Tom Peterson** headed marketing and communications at **Heifer International** for almost two decades. Under his leadership annual marketing revenue grew from $3 million in 1992 to $90 million in 2008. Peterson and team turned a low-performing fundraising program—the gift catalog that Heifer innovated—into one that is copied worldwide. Heifer was also an early leader in online fundraising. In naming Heifer nonprofit of the year the Direct Marketing Association said, "Heifer International has fundamentally redefined direct response humanitarian relief fundraising." During Peterson's tenure Heifer was featured in *The New York Times*, *Fast Company*, *The Oprah Winfrey Show*, CNN, 60 Minutes and *West Wing*. Peterson teaches marketing for nonprofits at the **Clinton School of Public Service** in Little Rock. Among other activities, he manages the communications for **Stakeholder Health**, a learning collaborative of health systems. In the 1980s, he edited *Seeds*, a magazine about U.S. and world hunger. Peterson graduated from the University of Texas and Austin Presbyterian Theological Seminary. Find more at **Cosmorock.org**.

CPSIA information can be obtained
at www.ICGtesting.com
Printed in the USA
BVHW040316030822
643590BV00001B/41